The Improvement Book

Creating the
Problem-free Workplace

Tomō Sugiyama

Foreword by Norman Bodek
President
Productivity, Inc.

Edited by
Japan Management Association

Productivity Press
CAMBRIDGE, MASSACHUSETTS
NORWALK, CONNECTICUT

The Improvement Book

Creating the
Problem-free Workplace

Originally published as *Genba kaizen no susumekata* by Japan Management Association, Tokyo, Japan. Copyright © 1988 by Japan Management Association.

English translation copyright © 1989 by Productivity, Inc.

Productivity Press
P.O. Box 3007
Cambridge, MA 02140
(617) 497-5146

Library of Congress Catalog Card Number: 89-61104
ISBN: 0-915299-47-X

Cover design by Donna Puleo
Typeset by Rudra Press, Cambridge, MA
Printed and bound by the Courier Book Companies
Printed in the United States of America

Library of Congress Cataloging-in-Publication Data

Sugiyama, Tomō, 1914–
Genba kaizen no susumekata.   English
   The improvement book: creating the problem-free workplace/Tomō Sugiyama.
   Translation of: *Genba kaizen no susumekata*/ Sugiyama Tomō.
   ISBN 0-915299-47-X
   1. Production management.   2. Industrial management.   I. Title.
   TS155.S86413   1989
   658.5'1-dc20   89-61104

89 90 91   10 9 8 7 6 5 4 3 2 1

Contents

List of Figures

Publisher's Foreword

The bounty of creative ideas from Japan never ceases to amaze me. At one time, we saw Japan as a nation of copiers. If it *was* true, it surely is not true today. Some of the most innovative production systems of this century have come from Japan, radically reshaping the international economy over the last 45 years.

It should be no surprise that some of the most creative ideas from Japan are about creativity itself — concepts that respect the ability of each employee, in whatever position, to contribute something to his or her job besides physical effort. Inviting people to *use* their creative abilities and their knowledge about their jobs creates an involved and satisfied workforce that wants to make the best products and give the best service.

This element of personal creativity has been developed in many American as well as Japanese companies in the form of quality circle programs. To promote individual participation as well as small group activities, we recently translated *The Idea Book*, an introduction to the Total Improvement Proposal System, or TIPS — a company-wide continual improvement suggestion system. The U.S. companies already using the TIPS concept are benefiting from a more involved and more satisfied workforce.

In this book, I am pleased to share with you another creative idea: Tomō Sugiyama's "problem-free engineering," a practical, down-to-earth variation of the TIPS concept.

Problem-free engineering is a problem-detecting and problem-solving method that involves everyone in the workplace. At the heart of it is a careful five-minute daily observation for instances of the "Big 3" workplace problems: irrationality, inconsistency, and waste. Even when they see no apparent problem situations, employees can use the elements of problem-free engineering as ideal standards to "create" problems to improve. They might ask, for example, "How can we make this job *walk-free* (eliminating unnecessary walking)?" or "We're wasting a lot of empty space on the storage shelves (*air-free*)." Using terms like these (and creating new ones as needed), problem-free engineering provides a framework of simple slang so everyone in the company can easily grasp the ideas and quickly move on to applying them.

The critical step is to write down the problems observed immediately, before they are forgotten, even if no solution comes to mind at the moment. The Big 3 Memo form provides an effective way to record information about the problem and eventual improvement plan, as well as the cost savings from a particular idea. In Japan, each employee keeps a personal workbook of these forms, which keeps them from being misplaced and provides useful tips and a log sheet for recording problems, dates, and money saved from making improvements. An example of the workbook is included at the end of this book. Reprints of the workbook for use in your own company may be ordered through Productivity Press.

This is a truly informative book, drawing on anecdotes and examples from the author's long career with the Yamaha company and his experiences with other companies using this system in Japan for dramatic savings. This is a valuable resource for first-line supervisors as well as middle and upper management people. The workbook and memo form are intended for hands-on use by *everyone* from production workers on up. Although the "problem-free" concept originated in manufacturing, Mr. Sugiyama has extended it with charts and examples for the office setting and for safety and energy concerns that apply to any type of organization.

The Improvement Book is a practical guide to actually setting up a participatory problem-solving system in the workplace. It provides clear directions for starting a problem-free engineering program, a full introduction to basic concepts of industrial housekeeping (known in Japan as 5S), and two chapters of examples that can be used in small group training activities. The memo form is designed to make it easy for every participant to express his or her creativity in identifying problems and developing solutions to improve the workplace.

The creative efforts of many people contributed to the English edition of *The Improvement Book*. I would like to thank Fred Czupryna, Alan Campbell, and George Smith for the translation; Karen Jones and Rosemary Winfield for editorial work; Sally Schwager for editorial translations and assistance with queries; Julie Zinkus and Elizabeth Sutherland for the index; Esmé McTighe for production; our friends at Rudra Press for typesetting and pasteup; and Donna Puleo for the cover design. We express special appreciation to Kazuya Uchiyama of Japan Management Association and to the author, Tomō Sugiyama, for their assistance in clarifying the English manuscript.

Norman Bodek
President
Productivity, Inc.

Editorial Note

The original Japanese edition of this book includes many references to cost savings in yen. In an effort to make these figures more meaningful to a western audience, we have converted the amounts to dollar values. In instances where the entire discussion took place during one year, the conversion rate for the first business day of the year was used. For situations involving more than one year, the arithmetic mean value of the rate at the beginning of each year was used. Generally, dollar amounts of three or more digits have been rounded to the nearest ten dollars and one to two-digit amounts to the nearest dollar.

The Improvement Book

Creating the
Problem-free Workplace

CHAPTER 1

The Meaning of Problem-free Engineering

A New Approach to Improvement Activities

Thirty years ago most people would not have known the meaning of the word "windsurfing." Today, most people immediately understand the word, and when they hear it they probably picture a person in a bathing suit cruising through waves on a fiberglass board with a colorful sail attached to it.

Some people complain about the corruption of the language with such new terms, but I believe language must change to express the culture of the times. To keep up with changing times, I recently coined a term to describe a workplace improvement method I was developing: "problem-free engineering."

Problem-free engineering is an approach that aims at reducing the three basic problems★ of the workplace — irrationality, inconsistency, and waste — to zero. Of the four basic principles of workplace improvement — eliminate, combine, rearrange, and simplify — the most effective is eliminate. Ultimately, "to eliminate" simply means to stop doing what does not need to be done. Problem-free engineering means striving for improvement based on the fundamental idea that irrationality, inconsistency, and waste can be eliminated or at least reduced significantly.

The basic elements of problem-free engineering can be expressed by completing the expression " _-free engineering" with some irrationality, inconsistency, or waste that occurs in the workplace. "Walk-free" engineering (eliminating excess walking) and "conveyor-free" engineering (eliminating unnecessary use of conveyors) are two examples.

★ "Three basic problems" is a translation of three Japanese words for workplace problems, often referred to together as *3 M* or *3 Mu*: *muri* (irrationality), *mura* (inconsistency), and *muda* (waste). The Japanese syllable *mu* is a negative prefix similar to the English "ir-" or "in-." In this book, the term "Big 3" is generally used for these words. "Engineering" in this context is used broadly to include not only industrial engineering but also improvement activities and quality control methods in general. — Ed.

The applications of this concept are limited only by the imagination, making it a helpful tool for attacking and rooting out all kinds of waste. These terms are shorthand expressions that all employees can pick up and immediately grasp.

Sociological research has shown that using this type of catch-phrase or buzzword to popularize an idea within a company can be very effective in focusing a companywide improvement effort. For example, if you use Toyota production system terminology such as "kanban," "just-in-time," or "production leveling" with someone who is also familiar with these terms, the set of ideas that they invoke helps the listener quickly understand what you mean. This makes it possible to proceed directly to higher-level discussion, questions, and answers.

Some people believe that the Apollo space program owed its success to NASA's in-house slang vocabulary, which made it easy for workers to talk about concepts everyone understood. The use of problem-free engineering and various " -free" phrases also contributes to a common language for the entire company. If the terms express universal factors, they can help promote understanding of waste and implementation of waste-reducing activities throughout the entire company. Chapters 6 and 7 give examples of some of the many improvement ideas that have come from the application of these concepts.

Origins and Background
Beginning with "Air-free" Engineering

During the 1973 oil shock I was production manager at Yamaha Motor and one day I found myself staring intently at the shelves of parts stored in the warehouse. The shelves were arranged thoughtlessly, with much unused space above the parts. A similar space waste occurred when the transport carts were loaded. Although signs placed throughout the warehouse urged workers "Don't store air!" and "Don't transport air!" people just weren't following them. There must have been a vague awareness that storage methods could be improved: someone did post the signs directly in front of the parts shelves.

After a while a production technology engineer and his boss came to where I was standing, curious about what I was looking at. "I'm concerned about the unused space over the parts shelves. I wonder if anything can be done about it," I said. "Well, there really is a lot of empty space, isn't there?" they noted. "We'll take a look at it."

We had this conversation at about 5 p.m., but by the next day I had forgotten about it completely. When I came to work in the morning, I was surprised to find the engineer and the manager waiting for me on the plant floor. They asked me to look at what they had come up with after studying the situation and working until 9 p.m.

In a few hours, they had reduced the space between the parts shelves to the minimum needed to retrieve things. They also rearranged the parts, lining them up in a more rational and systematic way. The result, shown in Figure 1-1, was that they had "created" 35 percent more space, which before had been wasted.

Figure 1-1. The Origin of "Air-free Engineering"

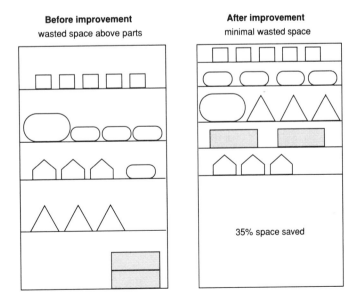

This improvement intrigued me. At that moment, the concept of problem-free engineering was born. Eventually that concept expanded to include all improvement activities.

I had always been aware of the waste resulting from unused space, but the way these employees created more storage space led me to a breakthrough development in solving problems in the workplace. If it was possible to rearrange space rationally, more space would naturally become available for use. Many managers complain that their factories don't have enough space. With a little imagination, however, I was able to come up with outrageous ideas to "create" space, so that it became clear that we might get along without building new factories.

But it is not effective to have only a few workers apply partial solutions to waste problems here and there. The only effective way to make improvements is to promote activities in which everyone throughout the company participates. Once the entire company is involved, it is easy to use a common language to communicate ideas about improvements.

As a result of the warehouse rearrangement, we began to use the term "air-free engineering" as shorthand for "don't store surplus air where you could store something that you need to store." Soon everyone in the company understood what we meant when we used the term. Furthermore, a special term like "air-free engineering" confers distinction on an important activity.

The term I coined made it easier to implement solutions with a minimum of detailed discussion and explanation. Although many people at first thought the term sounded a bit strange, I asked them to indulge me and kept on using it.

At first, I made attempts to get people in the company to think of me as "Air-free Sugiyama" or "Sugiyama the Air-free." Even when only a few people were listening, I worked in the term "air-free" in conversation, using a self-styled evangelism to promote the term and the activities it represents. As a result, some fruits of my effort began to appear throughout the company.

"Bolt-free" Engineering

While air-free engineering was gradually spreading through the company, I had a chance to observe closely some assembly operations at one plant. The late Kaichi Kawakami, chairman of Nippon Gakki (the predecessor of Yamaha Ltd.), once advised me: "Observe the work that requires the most people for the same operation!"

I thought a lot about this advice and really let it sink in. Assembly operations for motorcycle bodies are operations that require a large number of workers. One idea I kept thinking about was reducing the number of workers by automating assembly or using robots.

As I watched the assembly operations, I soon noticed that the most basic operation, regardless of part, was fastening bolts with nuts. There were several kinds of nuts and bolts, but all required some action to fasten them together.

I compared how many bolts were used for each motorcycle and what kinds were used for each. The number of workers doing the assembling seemed to be in perfect direct proportion to the number of bolts used for assembly within the company, as shown in the correlation diagram (see Figure 1-2).

As I thought about using robots and automation to reduce the labor cost for all this bolt fastening, it occurred to me to question whether we really needed as many bolts as we were using.

Figure 1-2. "Bolt-free Engineering"
(relation between the number of bolts and the number
of assembly workers)

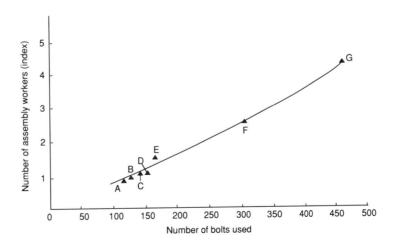

Were some not functional? If we could eliminate unnecessary bolts, a significant labor savings would result. I believed this situation deserved a careful study.

To do this, I applied the "air-free" idea to reduce the number of bolts to the minimum number required. Soon people around the company started talking about "bolt-free engineering" and popularizing this idea with posters and activities. After seeing the "air-free" idea transferred to another workplace problem, people began generating other "   -free engineering" ideas, sparking a further expansion of problem-free engineering.

Detecting Waste with Problem-free Engineering

Waste is probably the most pervasive of the three basic workplace problems; things that are inconsistent or irrational frequently are wasteful as well. The first objective of problem-free engineering is to help employees learn to perceive wastefulness in the workplace. If you can perceive waste, you can start to come up with ideas about eliminating or reducing it. These ideas become the basis of improvement suggestions such as the ones recorded on a Big 3 Memo (named for the three basic problems).

The Toyota production system singles out seven kinds of waste in the workplace:

- Waste from overproduction
- Waste from waiting
- Waste from transporting
- Waste in the processing itself
- Waste in inventory
- Waste in operations
- Waste from defects

To eliminate waste, you must first study the actual situation to identify waste and then determine how to eliminate or reduce it. Detecting waste is easiest when you make observations with a clear picture of how things should be. Problem-free engineering provides such a standard in observing your work area for waste: a smooth-running and trouble-free workplace.

The object of problem-free engineering is to stop doing things inefficiently. Anything done indifferently or inefficiently must be seen as "waste," no matter how much effort may be put into it.

One attractive feature of this approach is that it doesn't cost any money. The payback derived from working toward an accident-free workplace is eliminating safety risks, and striving for "zero defects" eliminates causes of poor quality. Savings do not stop with the one-time elimination of waste.

This doesn't mean, however, that no money will need to be spent. Some countermeasure engineering is required — a basic investment in getting equipment in peak operating condition. You must attack from the hardware (equipment) front as well as the software (engineering) front.

The important focus is on eliminating waste and stopping wasteful activity, but be careful not to make superficial, short-term changes. The objective of a workplace improvement program such as problem-free engineering is to detect and solve problems at their source.

Problem-free Engineering and Problem-solving

No matter how much excitement is generated at the beginning, improvement activities won't get off the ground unless an easy-to-use problem-solving method helps people keep the concepts in mind during their working day. The Big 3 Memo is the technique we have developed for carrying out problem-free engineering in the workplace. Chapters 4 and 5 discuss this technique in depth, and examples of actual memos appear in Chapter 7.

Because not much has been written about how to use problem-free engineering in problem-solving, I asked Professor Kazuho Yoshimoto of the Waseda University Department of Engineering and Industrial Management and Norio Suzuki of the Yamaha Motor Co. industrial engineering staff to write an article organizing some of these concepts. The following material is adapted from their article, "Improving the Worksite with ' -free Engineering' and the Big 3 Memo," from the December 1984 issue of *Factory Management* magazine. I present it here as a brief introduction to basic problem-solving concepts as they relate to the Big 3 Memo.

What Is a "Problem"?

The starting point for worksite improvement activities is an accurate grasp of existing problems. Leaders assist with implementing the improvements, and the quality of the results rests on their commitment and ability. When problems are not grasped accurately (for example, when people are too close to their work to see limiting conditions), subsequent improvement activities will not be as effective as they could be.

What kinds of things should be called "problems"? A problem can be defined as "any deviation from a standard." Standards can be generally classified into two groups: *established standards* and *desired standards*. Established standards are realistic targets resulting from evaluation of the current regular situation. Desired standards are higher and more idealistic goals that result from dissatisfaction with current established standards. Their relationship is shown in Figure 1-3.

Here are some examples of problems caused by deviation from established standards:

- The average defect rate three months ago was 2 percent, but yesterday's production lots had a 6 percent defect rate.

Figure 1-3. Problems as Deviations from Standards

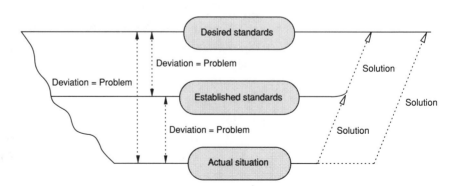

- Management's goal is no more than three cases of late delivery per month, but six cases were late this month.
- The goal is a failure shutdown rate of no more than 2 percent, but the total for last week was 5 percent.

Problems like these are generally deviations from established standards. Such problems can be solved by identifying their causes so that the situation can be returned to normal. Problem-solving is therefore a matter of changing a deviation from standard situation back to a standard situation.

Solving problems at the worksite involves correcting deviations from established standards, but simply returning to an established standard will cause the improvement to remain superficial. To achieve a desired standard, more fundamental improvements must be made.

Before you can identify and correct deviations from a desired standard, you must first define what that standard is. A "desired standard" means

- The way things should really be
- The most desirable situation
- A situation that is hoped for

A problem caused by deviation from a desired standard, therefore, is a discrepancy between the actual established situation and the way things should really be.

Here are some examples of deviation of an established standard from a desired standard:

- The desired standard is zero defects, but management's target is a 2 percent defect rate.
- The desired standard is zero late deliveries, but management's goal is no more than three late deliveries.
- The desired standard is zero failure shutdowns, but management's target is a failure shutdown rate of no more than 2 percent.

What Type of Problem Do You Have?

Problems with the five production factors

Figure 1-4 shows the relationship of the five basic factors that transform raw materials into manufactured products. Each of these factors has its own concrete problems as well as problems with the other factors. Some of the concrete problems are

- Defective materials
- Unskilled operation, waiting, poor work conditions
- Frequent machine breakdown, idleness, and deterioration
- Obsolete work methods
- Energy waste
- High operator to equipment ratios
- Low yield rate for machinery and materials

Problems based on customer demand

Customers have three main demands from manufactured products:

- High quality (Q)
- Reasonable price (P)
- On-time delivery (D)

All three factors should be studied. No matter how high the quality or how low the price, if a product is not delivered when the customer wants it, it will not succeed in the marketplace. Ask the following questions when you evaluate your product:

- Do you receive many complaints about quality?
- Do you incur many delivery delays?
- Are you losing market share because of high costs?

By investigating the causes of such problems, you can plan solutions in the areas that need improvement.

Problems based on elements of workplace management

There are six basic elements of workplace management:

- Productivity (P)
- Quality (Q)
- Cost (C)
- Delivery (D)
- Safety (S)
- Morale (M)

Figure 1-4. The Five Production Factors

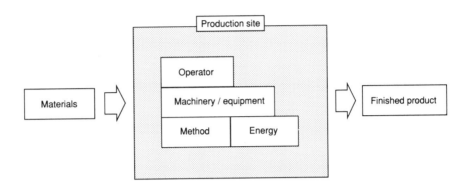

Use these categories to help you discover situations that can be improved in the workplace. For example:

- Hourly productivity has fallen from last month's rate (P)
- The defect rate exceeds management's limits (Q)
- Scheduled delivery dates are not met (D)
- Workplace accidents have increased during the last few days (S)

Problem detection will become easier when you use these elements to collect and organize data from your work area. By going through these categories, it will become clearer which direction your improvement efforts should take.

How to Detect Problems

Problems that just happen; "created" problems

A "problem" has been defined as any discrepancy (deviation) between the actual situation and established standards or desired standards. On the production floor, established standards tend to fall under one of the six elements of management just described (P, Q, C, D, S, M). Workplace problems that involve deviations from established standards usually "just happen," and when they do, the situation is studied to find the cause.

Many other problems in the workplace do not have standards to be compared against. For example, sudden breakdowns can occur, production can begin under untried new conditions, new products can be developed, and so on. In such cases the problem cannot be grasped accurately because there *is* no established standard. To define the problem, a desired standard is formulated to reflect the ideal situation. Comparing the desired standard with the actual situation "creates" the problem.

Setting the level of expectation

As Figure 1-3 shows, the most inclusive group of problems is the gap between desired standards and the actual situation. In the daily routine it is easy to overlook deviations from even the established standards. However, setting a higher goal — a desired standard — can sometimes bring a fresh new approach to problem detection.

What level of expectation should be developed for desired standards? If the objective is to uncover problems for the sake of improvement activities, two types of desired standards can be considered. One is the "real standard," which reflects the ideal situation under limited conditions. This is always a higher standard than the established standard. Another way is the "temporary standard," reflecting the ideal situation without any limitation.

Figure 1-5 shows the relationships among the actual situation, the established standard, the real standard, and the temporary standard. To decide the real standard, consider an ideal situation that can actually be achieved, taking into account such limitations as technical feasibility, the amount to be invested, time period, and so on. Determining the real standard takes some time and research.

Figure 1-5. Temporary and Real Standards

Problem-free engineering creates temporary standards

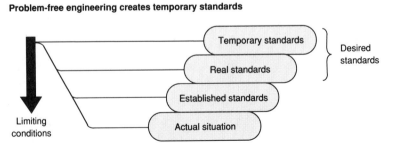

With a temporary standard, you don't have to consider any limiting conditions, so you can apply it and see results right away. The "problem-free engineering" approach proposed by Tomō Sugiyama as a director of Yamaha Motor is an example of using temporary standards for workplace improvement.

"Problem-free engineering" means having a production site where everyone works toward the "temporary" goal of totally eliminating the three basic problems of irrationality, inconsistency, and waste. This results from applying the concepts of "completely" and " -free" to express temporary standards as improvement goals and observing carefully for ways in which the present condition deviates from these standards. By means of the Big 3 Memo, these concepts guide problem detection as well as improvement activities.

Figure 1-6. Examples of Problem-free Engineering

Factory management

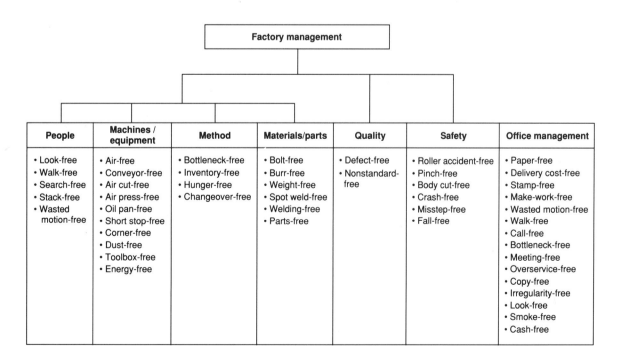

People	Machines / equipment	Method	Materials/parts	Quality	Safety	Office management
• Look-free	• Air-free	• Bottleneck-free	• Bolt-free	• Defect-free	• Roller accident-free	• Paper-free
• Walk-free	• Conveyor-free	• Inventory-free	• Burr-free	• Nonstandard-free	• Pinch-free	• Delivery cost-free
• Search-free	• Air cut-free	• Hunger-free	• Weight-free		• Body cut-free	• Stamp-free
• Stack-free	• Air press-free	• Changeover-free	• Spot weld-free		• Crash-free	• Make-work-free
• Wasted motion-free	• Oil pan-free		• Welding-free		• Misstep-free	• Wasted motion-free
	• Short stop-free		• Parts-free		• Fall-free	• Walk-free
	• Corner-free					• Call-free
	• Dust-free					• Bottleneck-free
	• Toolbox-free					• Meeting-free
	• Energy-free					• Overservice-free
						• Copy-free
						• Irregularity-free
						• Look-free
						• Smoke-free
						• Cash-free

Detecting Problems with the Big 3 Memo

What is the main reason that an improvement suggestion system does not continue smoothly or that it is not effective enough? The most frequent response in many workplaces is that the suggesters find it too troublesome to make improvement plans and to take responsibility for following through until implementation and results are achieved.

To establish a foundation for workplace improvement activities, the first step should be observation to detect problems. Workplace conditions should then be considered from the perspective of a desired, temporary standard — "How can we make this workplace 'problem-free'?" — with no pressure to plan, implement, or achieve improvements. The vehicle for writing down problems observed in the workplace is the Big 3 Memo.

Next, those things that are similar are combined and arranged so that the real causes of problems can be analyzed. This information is then considered in relation to improvement activities. Problem detection is therefore extremely effective when done from a perspective of "problem-free engineering," using the Big 3 Memo in the context of Q-C-D and P-Q-C-D-S-M.

The Problem-free Engineering Approach to Problem-solving

Using the problem-free engineering approach will greatly increase the fruits of improvement, fruits that could not grow in the past because of attitudes such as "We've always done it this way," or "There is no other option." Possibilities for effective planning for improvement will also be significantly expanded.

The Big 3 Memo is an effective way to use the problem-free engineering approach to observe and record problems from a desired standard perspective. A number of companies and production areas have been conducting improvement activities using problem-free engineering and the Big 3 Memo for several years now. We had not realized that observing and listing problems could record so much information as well as give peace of mind. Using industrial engineering methods to solve such problems can promote highly efficient improvement activities with objective analysis and investigation.

"Winning is sometimes a matter of luck, but losing is not. The causes of problems are not matters of luck or accident. There is always room for improvement!"

CHAPTER 2

Methods for Promoting Workplace Improvement

Target: Places Where Many People Do the Same Thing

After World War II food and other necessities were scarce throughout Japan, and people worked to restore the country's devastated and disorganized industries. Nippon Gakki Co. (the parent company of Yamaha Motor) supplied propellers during the war and was heavily damaged. With great effort, its leaders restored the company to peacetime work, concentrating on pre-war expertise in furniture products and musical instruments.

During that period I was in charge of machinery in the lumber section of the woodworking division. I repaired fire-damaged machinery and struggled to make improvements while learning how to run a woodwork processing operation. One day the company president, the late Kaichi Kawakami, came to observe our shop. After listening to our reports, he gave us some of his own ideas about improving the workplace. I can still picture him, wearing his hat but no dust mask, as the sawdust floated around him. His face was kind, but behind his glasses his eyes were determined. What he said has significance for me even today.

After staring intently at the running machines, Mr. Kawakami suddenly asked me, "When you want to improve a workplace, what areas do you pay special attention to?" I didn't know how to answer this sudden question. He continued: "When you are trying to improve something, look for places where a lot of workers are doing the same job. If you do, you will find that even small improvements will yield big results."

One of the operations in my shop involved a hand-held planer for smoothing the wood. Like a circular saw, it is a general purpose machine with high adaptability and is indispensable for any woodworking shop.

At the time 30 of these machines were operating in one place — an impressive sight. When the machines were arranged in the order in which they were to be used, it occurred to me that the workpieces could be transferred between machines mechanically, freeing the workers from having to load and unload. To study this idea, I read a journal specializing in advanced American woodworking operations, but it dealt only with more advanced techniques and did not address my problem. I wondered if anyone was using automatic conveyors for machines such as ripsaws, leveling planers, and glue jointers.

Certainly no one was producing these machines yet in Japan. With Mr. Kawakami's permission, however, I commissioned K Ironworks to develop some experimental models and guaranteed that I would accept responsibility for any risks. Within a year, we were able to switch over gradually to automatic conveyors. With this innovation, we were able to accomplish with only seven machines what used to require 30, which led to reduced labor costs for those operations, more efficient use of space, and a safer workplace.

By starting with the simple rule of looking closer at situations where many people perform the same operations, you will certainly be able to locate a starting point for improvements.

Even Small Improvements Yield Big Results

The two basic methods for improving manufacturing plants have their own special features. Figure 2-1 gives a graphic comparison of the two methods.

The first method (see A in the figure) is called "innovative improvement." This achieves greater efficiency by making improvements and concentrating large investments of money and personnel on individual, designated areas. Some examples of this include automation, the use of robots, flexible manufacturing systems (FMS), development of new processing methods, improvement of production methods, and new materials and products. Companies that advance in this direction have become leaders in the industrial world.

Every workplace, however, also has a "horizontal" dimension consisting of the compound effect of many people and many machines working together every day. This horizontal factor gives the workplace a life of its own. If this factor is ignored, many kinds of waste will be allowed to exist throughout the company.

The reverse is also true: relatively small improvements from each person can produce a large savings in the end. Even problems and waste that might seem too insignificant to bother

Figure 2-1. Methods for Promoting Improvement Activities

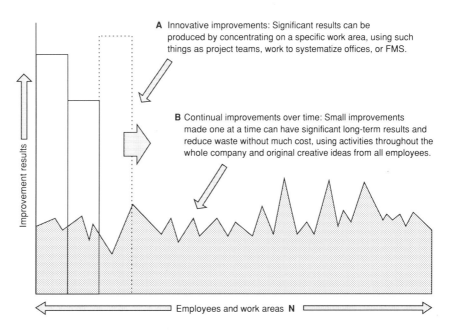

with become important when many people are involved in solving the problems they observe around them.

In order to get the maximum result from improvement activities, a company needs to find a way to involve every person in the company. Small group activities and workers' original improvement proposals are two effective ways to promote "problem consciousness" throughout the company. The improvement activities that evolve from the Big 3 Memo system are especially beneficial because they can be used by everyone, from top management and company directors to hourly employees.

Another way to picture the two types of improvement activities is the example of an ancient stone wall built without mortar (see Figure 2-2). From a distance, the wall looks solid, with large pieces of rock carefully fitted together. As you look closer, however, you see that large gaps exist between the big rocks. What gives the wall its strength and solid appearance are the many small stones that are carefully placed in the gaps, "fine-tuning" the fit of the large stones.

Figure 2-2. A Strong Wall Needs Large and Small Stones

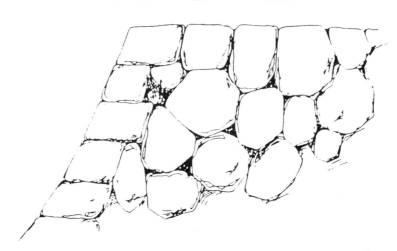

You cannot build a strong wall by stacking only large rocks.
Strength comes from the many small stones that fill in the gaps.

If you look at the innovative improvements into which a company pours its organizational talent, capital, and personnel as "big rocks," you will see the gaps there too — the many instances of waste that you have to look closely to see. Like the small stones in the wall, the ideas and activities that fill these gaps make a strong and solid whole of a company's improvement strategy.

Giving Up Comfortable Reliance on Fixed Ideas

When you carefully investigate the reasons that improvement activities in the workplace often do not lead to the progress or involvement that was anticipated, you frequently discover that people tend to fall into comfortable, stereotyped views of their environments. Furthermore, most people are not even aware that they have these preconceptions.

Examples of Fixed Ideas

To make improvements, people have to become aware of their stereotyped views of things. I like to use a simple exercise I learned from Professor Yoshimoto. First, ask participants to draw a ten-dollar bill from memory. Then ask them to name the person they have drawn and the picture on the back. In a typical group,

- 10% can draw the correct dimensions.
- 10 to 20% can sketch or describe the pictures.
- Only 3% can do both things correctly.

Even though people handle and look at ten-dollar bills all the time, these details don't register because no one has any special relationship to either the size of the bill or the person or place shown on it.

The importance of a bill to most people is the amount it is worth: *this* distinguishes a ten from a one or a twenty. To most people, everything else is just something the government has done to decorate it. In using a bill at face value without noticing its details, people are not really observing it.

It is just as easy to unquestioningly accept habitual patterns in work situations. A certain workplace I used to pass always had a truck parked outside. Figure 2-3 (before improvement) shows the route workers took to load and unload the truck. One day I asked one of the workers about it.

"Doing all that walking to load and unload is really quite a hassle isn't it?"

"It sure is!"

"Isn't there some way you could do the job without all this walking?"

The worker looked at me as though it had never crossed his mind.

"Well," I said, "What if you parked the truck facing the other way?"

"That might be a good idea. It would cut down the walking distance, wouldn't it?"

"Why is it parked facing this way?"

"Someone decided a long time ago that this is how it should be parked."

"Who made that decision?"

"Gee, I don't know. That's just the way we've always done it."

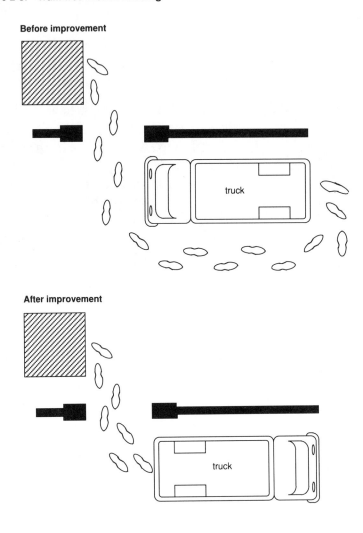

Figure 2-3. "Walk-free" Truck Loading

These workers and their supervisor were doing the job the way they had always done it without noticing that there might be another, easier approach. After our conversation, they parked the trucks the other way to minimize the walking distance. Using the Big 3 Memo is a great way to wake people from this type of complacency and get them to see the waste in the situations around them.

Using 5W1H

I'm not kidding, I have seen the sun rise in the west. Are you curious to know more? If you really want to know, you might start asking me questions about it.

"Okay, *where* did you see that?" — "In Florida."

"*Whereabouts* in Florida?" — "At an airport in Florida."

"About *what time* was it?" — "At dusk."

"What was your *situation* at that time?" — "My plane had just taken off."

"Can you give me some more details about *why* the sun rose from the west?" — "When the plane took off, the sun had just set in the west. While the plane was climbing, the sun reappeared, coming up over the western horizon just like a sunrise. Surprising, isn't it? Then the plane banked to fly north and in a while I saw the sun set a second time."

"Well then," you will probably respond, "isn't it true that the sun only *appeared* to rise from the west but did not actually 'rise'?"

"That's right," I would answer. "But when you get right down to it, the sun only *appears* to rise in the east and set in the west. We have just become accustomed to calling it a sunrise or sunset."

The object of this dialogue is to draw you into a variation of the Twenty Questions game known as "5W1H." This exercise requires the listener to collect information about different aspects of a situation in order to make sense of it. By asking some of the questions of 5W1H — "when," "where," "what," and "why" (see Figure 2-4), the listener learns about my actual situation in Florida as well as his or her own comfortable reliance on accepted misconceptions about the sun's "rising" and "setting."

5W1H is an important tool that develops the complete facts of a situation and then examines the reasons for them. Reporters use this technique every day to get the facts for news articles. It is useful in any situation that needs to be understood more concretely.

Meetings, for example, can drag on with hours of discussion and debate, but participants often fail to reach conclusions or plans of action. Many of these meetings remain at an abstract level from beginning to end. Using the framework of the 5W1H

Figure 2-4. Five W's and One H

5W1H		Questions
WHAT	What for? (Purpose)	• What is that? • What is it for? • What would happen if that operation were eliminated? • What else should be done?
WHY	Why? (Necessity)	• Why is that being done? • Why is that necessary? • Why that way?
WHERE	Where? (Place)	• Where is the location? • Why there? • Can things be combined in one place? • Should the location be changed?
WHEN	When? (Sequence)	• When was that? • Why was it done at that time? • When is the most reasonable time to do it? • Can it be done at another time?
WHO	Who? (Operator)	• Who is that? • Why does that person do that operation? • Does the job require special qualifications? • Are many people doing the same job?
HOW	How? (Method)	• Why is it being done this way? • Is that the best way to do it? • Can it be done another way? • How much will it cost?

approach effectively turns abstract arguments into concrete debates. 5W1H can be used throughout the company to focus the problem-solving process to achieve concrete solutions.

Essential Tools for Analyzing the Actual Condition

During a hospital stay I made an interesting observation: even when doctors don't ask their patients many questions, they manage to do their jobs quite well. Nurses take a detailed history and make appropriate entries in the patient's record. They also check temperature, respiration, and pulse. When necessary, technicians carry out blood tests, X-ray examinations, and urine analyses and enter these results in the record.

When doctors make rounds, they do not have to spend a lot of time interviewing patients. With the information in the record, doctors can use their knowledge and expertise to make appropriate decisions for treatment.

Problem-free engineering for the workplace is actually a lot like medical treatment. Many people make careful observations, ask the 5W1H questions about the facts of the situation, and then note their observations in a record — the Big 3 Memo. Later, they record the "treatment" or improvement in the Memo. It is important to have a firm grasp of the facts of the situation to avoid making mistakes.

Using 5W1H to Analyze the Actual Condition

Understand the facts just as they are

Getting a real grasp of the facts — the true situation — is not as easy as it sounds. It is necessary to expose and eliminate our hidden preconceptions — the fixed ideas we usually don't even think about. Making decisions on the basis of conjecture must be avoided at all costs.

Be objective

Being subjective means setting yourself as the standard of judgment when thinking about things, considering how to make things turn out conveniently for your own advantage. Being objective requires you to set aside personal opinions and preferences and view the facts from the perspective of the improvement of the situation as a whole. You must correct your own misunderstanding and carry out decisions with everyone's interests in mind.

Grasp things quantitatively

Being abstract means being separated from the reality of things so that you lack a clear understanding of the content. The word "concrete" means just the opposite. The 5W1H approach is a helpful method for expressing things concretely. Problems can be resolved more effectively when you have actual figures for questions like "how much?" or "how many?"

Check for mistakes

You can avoid mistakes by doing things conscientiously, double-checking, and considering situations from many different perspectives.

Use symbols and graphs

Symbols and graphs should be used as much as possible because they can be understood immediately with few words. Think of the symbols on the television weather map that tell most of the story without the meteorologist's comments. A graph or a picture

- Makes everything understandable at a glance
- Gives all workers the same frame of reference
- Appeals to people's visual sense
- Enables the presenter to easily explain and persuade with just a few words

A solid grasp of these elements and constant application of 5W1H will help workplace activities improve immensely.

The Ultimate Weapon: The "5 Whys"

In problem-solving activities at the Toyota Motor Company, workers are encouraged to ask the question "why?" five times. This is an effective weapon for attacking waste at its origin. Repeating the question five times helps workers understand the root cause problem, so that the solution eliminates the problem and does not just treat its superficial symptoms.

An automatic welding machine operator gave me an example of how he used the 5 Whys in making observations for a Big 3 Memo. He had stopped the machine, as he often had to, and was thinking about why he had to go to that trouble and how to make the situation "stop-free."

Q: Why have you stopped the machine?
A: I'm sorting out the parts to be processed.
Q: Why are you sorting them out?
A: Because some of them deviate from the standard for this line.

Q: Why can't the deviations be allowed?

A: Parts with different dimensions cause welding defects.

Q: Why do you have to take care of it at this point, even having to stop the machine?

A: This wouldn't have to happen if we were getting good parts from the supplier.

Q: Why are these nonstandard parts delivered for processing in the first place?

A: They aren't being caught by the receiving inspection people.

This worker's questions and answers led to further investigation. When parts were put in storage they were later delivered uninspected, with quality standards not clearly defined. When the standard was defined and inspections were carried out, the defective parts didn't get through and the worker no longer had to stop the machine to sort each batch before processing. The situation was improved because the worker thought to use the 5 Whys to get at the cause of the problems.

Studying the Root Cause: The Heart of Improvement

Turning a Weak Point to Advantage

Some time ago I watched a television drama on the life of Ieyasu Tokugawa, the great military leader and shogun of the late sixteenth century. One aspect of the drama that impressed me deeply was the story of the battle of Nagashino, where Nobunaga Oda, using thousands of matchlock guns, combined forces with Ieyasu to defeat Katsuyori Takeda's traditionally armed cavalry.

The interesting thing here is the battle strategy Nobunaga devised. Guns were new and powerful weapons for that time, but loading them took longer than firing arrows. While they reloaded, the riflemen were exposed to enemy arrows and the other army could easily advance.

To deal with this situation, Nobunaga first had his soldiers build stockades against the Takeda cavalry. Then Nobunaga addressed the root cause of the problem. Knowing that the Takeda

Figure 2-5. Strategy of the Battle of Nagashino

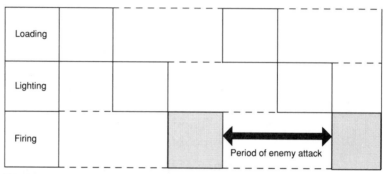

Takeda's thinking (limited to common sense)

Nobunaga's thinking (beyond common sense to innovation)

forces would expect lulls in fire during reloading, he divided the rifle brigade into three sections so that at all times one section was firing while the other two continually reloaded and lit the fuse. Figure 2-5 shows the strategy that led to Nobunaga's victory.

The key point for victory in this battle was that Nobunaga did not accept a weak point in his plan but thought carefully about what would win the battle. Realizing the importance of continuously firing on the enemy, Nobunaga devised a way to turn a weak point — the reloading cycle — to his own advantage. Using his resources with as little loss as possible, he defeated the opposing forces.

A remarkable parallel exists between Nobunaga's famous strategy and the way modern companies are improving their competitiveness by implementing just-in-time production. A just-in-time system requires a shift from large-lot production to leveled production, in which operations are synchronized to promote a continuous flow (see Figure 2-6). Like Nobunaga's army, the production-leveled factory is continually "firing" at the appropriate time. This system eliminates the expense. of maintaining inventory at any stage of the process: the parts are ready when needed for assembly, and the finished product comes off the line when it is ordered.

Figure 2-6. Effects of Production Leveling

Before improvement

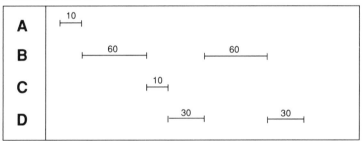

After improvement

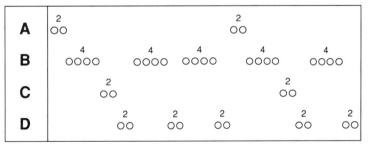

Effectiveness

    1. Absorbing imbalance between operator load leveling and number of workers for different machines

    2. Subassembly 1-unit flow ⎫
                               ⎬ Reduced personnel requirements
    3. Filling device load leveling ⎭

    4. Stock area reduction: from 60m ^{2} to 14m ^{2} (Δ75%)

Successful just-in-time implementation includes a number of specific improvement activities, such as improving hourly output and reducing changeover time. But like Nobunaga's guns, these activities themselves won't win the day. Finding a strategy for meshing them together effectively is the key to producing a level flow on the assembly line.

Lessons from Pompeii

During a visit to Italy, I was intrigued by the ruins of Pompeii. It is extraordinary to see evidence of towns and people buried 2000 years ago by the great eruption of Mt. Vesuvius. I noticed how the paved stone roads were built with separate areas for pedestrians and for vehicles (see Figure 2-7). The wheel tracks etched into the roadway were evidence of the prosperity that existed before the eruption.

The guide pointed out a square, 20-centimeter stone that jutted into the roadway (shown as A in the figure). "What do you think this is?" she asked. Everyone took a stab at it, but no one could figure it out. The guide explained that the stone was used to keep horse-drawn vehicles from moving. When we asked how a single stone could accomplish this, she pointed out that horses always go forward, never backward. Therefore, placing just one of these wheel blocks in front of a wheel was enough to keep the vehicle stopped.

The explanation of this simple device impressed me a great deal. Modern problem-solvers likewise need to learn to grasp the essence of the situation and find a simple way to deal with it.

Get to the Heart of the Problem

As you think about your own work situation and wonder whether your improvement efforts are getting to the real heart of the problem, you may find that your countermeasures do not strike at the root causes of problems.

The increasing popularity of 5S programs sometimes creates examples of superficial solutions.* Although the recent trend in many factories and workplaces to implement 5S is in principle an excellent goal, sometimes it mistakenly serves to mask problems rather than expose them.

---

* Chapter 3 deals with 5S, or basic principles of industrial housekeeping. — Ed.

Figure 2-7. Road in Pompeii

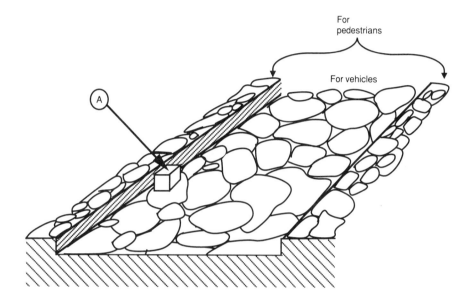

In many companies, for example, I have seen people sprucing up passageways with new paint. But does it occur to anyone that simply painting a dirty passageway may not be a good thing? I once asked this question in a seminar. People answered at first that it seemed like a good thing to renovate and repaint. But then they started to have some doubts and raised questions such as "How much will this cost?" and "Well, why is it necessary?"

Then the questions shifted to things like "Who is making the passageways dirty?" and "Shouldn't we check this out a little more?" Closer observation revealed that the forklift made black tire marks on the passageways, which was why repainting was suggested. It seemed unlikely that just painting them over would result in a permanent improvement.

The seminar group observed the situation and noticed these things:

- There were two types of forklifts, engine-powered and battery-powered. A comparison showed that the battery type was less likely to leave marks.

- Sudden starts and stops made most of the tire marks.
- The tires themselves were dirty.

The proposal for dealing with the essence of the problem included adopting a new standard of avoiding sudden stops and starts, with reminder notes painted on the forklifts. The tires were to be cleaned frequently, and a commitment was made to check the situation from time to time to make sure the new standard was working.

As this example shows, a superficial application of 5S will not attack the heart of the problem. Before you invest in an improvement activity, observe the situation carefully and discover the cause of the problem.

5S: The First Priority

One of the improvement terms heard most frequently in Japan is "5S." This is shorthand for five Japanese words beginning with "S" that express four basic principles of industrial housekeeping — putting in order, proper arrangement, cleaning, and purity (sometimes called 4S) — plus adherence or commitment (see Figure 3-1).* All kinds of businesses, offices, and workplaces are adopting the 5S approach.

Many companies are struggling with an increasingly competitive economic situation. Businesses strive for fundamental improvements and want the advantage of advanced management methods that can help their survival. 5S creates a companywide attitude of respect for the maintenance of the workplace and develops a set of activities to keep it running smoothly. This is one of the best methods for making any division more efficient. It is also a necessary foundation for any other improvement activity, including the problem-free engineering approach.

Using 5S activities in the workplace will improve the efficiency of the role of each member of a company, from top management down to the employees who perform the smallest details of operation. I would like to focus here on 5S improvement activities that apply to the production area itself, rather than the management aspect. Because many specialized books and articles provide detailed definitions, explanations, and methods of promoting 5S from a total productive maintenance (TPM) viewpoint, I am omitting such details from my discussion.**

---

 * A large number of Japanese companies use some form of 4S or 5S housekeeping program, although the definitions and constituent parts are defined uniquely by each organization. This book describes one variation. — Ed.

 ** For more information about total productive maintenance, see Seiichi Nakajima's books, *Introduction to TPM* (Productivity Press, 1988) and *TPM Development Program* (Productivity Press, 1989), and audiovisual training program, *TPM: Maximizing Productivity and Quality* (Productivity Press, 1989). — Ed.

Figure 3-1. The Elements of 5S

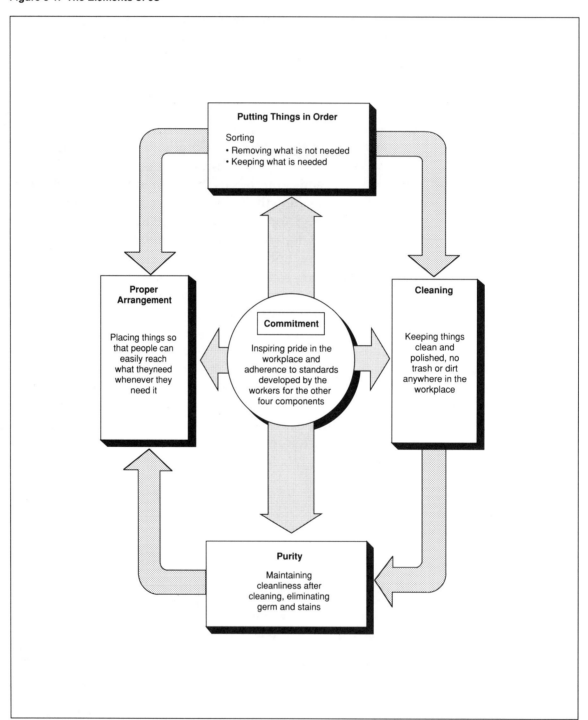

The Meaning of "5S"

In almost any factory you will see standard signs with pictures on them saying things like "Keep things in order and properly arranged!" or "Make the highest quality possible!" When you compare those signs with the work areas, however, you see that the slogans and pictures often have little to do with real life. Sometimes there is almost no relationship between the illustrations showing how to "order and arrange" and the way things are supposed to be. The signs may be interesting in terms of design, but one strains to guess why they were put there in the first place.

You can't apply 5S with stereotyped signs and slogans. 5S must be practical and practiced. It has to produce real and visible results that work for the actual situation. 5S cannot be implemented by just commanding workers to do it. Management has to lead the effort by demonstrating what it expects — and teaching everyone in the company why it is important. In too many cases, the company's 5S program is only window-dressing. As in a cartoon parade, the trumpet plays a loud fanfare and someone waves a banner, but the crowd is not following.

Management's most important task is to create a revolution in consciousness among the employees who are expected to implement 5S. "Consciousness revolution" might sound grandiose, but I use it because many problems are rooted in misunderstanding or failure to perceive things accurately. The following sections describe actions that management can use to change attitudes and promote understanding.

The Concept of 5S

Before workers can start doing 5S, they have to understand it. When you talk with people in the employee lounge and ask them "What is 5S?," their answers probably won't be very clear. The first essential step is teaching the basic elements. It is okay at first to deal with the general idea, but don't just hang up posters and think you have it covered. You have to provide daily training for employees. Begin a reading and discussion program and build understanding. Brief talks and discussion about 5S and TPM during regular morning meetings are a good way to start.

Why Is 5S Important?

From the beginning, group discussions centering on the question "Why do 5S?" will be more interesting and effective than learning rote answers. A coordinator can guide the discussion in the right direction and can consider it a success if opinions like the following emerge:

- We feel good when the place where we work every day is clean.
- We can avoid the hassle of searching for things.
- We can eliminate time wasted in handling.
- We can get along fine without buying unnecessary supplies.
- We can reduce our defect rate by detecting problems earlier.
- Our preventive maintenance will be better because equipment inspection will be easier.
- We can reduce the amount of machinery downtime and also increase the operation rate.
- We can create more usable space.
- Passageways can be kept clear and maintained better.
- Even small spaces can be used better.
- We can do just as well without new equipment we thought we had to have.
- We'll be able to spot abnormalities just by looking.
- Good housekeeping will help eliminate accidents and injuries.
- We want to show an attitude of pride and caring about the place where we work.
- We want to improve personal relations and promote a harmonious feeling among people who work together.
- If 5S goes well, anyone will be able to understand the situation at a glance.
- 5S is something everyone can do together.
- Total productivity is bound to increase.

Finally, a company's most precious asset is the trust of its customers and clients in the reliability of its products and processes. In countless companies, 5S improvements have been instrumental in winning the complete confidence of the customers, resulting in steady growth of the business.

Making the 5S Pledge

Once everyone understands the need for 5S and how effective it can be, you can begin to implement 5S improvement activities. In many Japanese companies, employees make a pledge at the beginning of the campaign to adhere to the standards of putting things in order, proper arrangement, cleaning, and purity they develop for the workplace. Everyone's signature is posted on the bulletin board as a symbol of their commitment and spirit to make their workplace the best it can be.

A 5S "Mirror": Fixed-point Photography

As was pointed out in Chapter 2, it is easy for people to go through their workdays comfortably feeling that everything is working all right and no problems need correction. In fact, usually many situations need to be remedied, but people just don't see them. Improvement begins with awareness of problems, and this awareness begins with cleanliness in the workplace.

The problem here is recognizing that there are problems. Workers, products, and workplaces all have them. But it is difficult for people to recognize their own shortcomings — or to see the problems where they work every day. In fact, trying to conceal our own negative points is a basic part of human nature.

People use mirrors to show them where their appearance needs correcting — messy hair or a smudge on the chin. A workplace also needs a "mirror" to reflect shortcomings. For this purpose we developed a method called "fixed-point photography" to reflect what needs to be improved.

Fixed-point photography is a method of repeatedly photographing a particular area of the workplace from the same position and facing the same direction, if possible with the same camera (see Figure 3-2). We photograph things we wouldn't want other people to see about the work area, the equipment, and the work methods. Special targets include

- Weaknesses in putting in order and arrangement (often in areas such as unsupervised power houses, cold-rooms, small parts storage, and document storage)

- Equipment and maintenance problems (oil leaks, unsafe places, and so on)
- Areas that waste energy

The value of fixed-point photography comes from the employees' involvement in the process. The workers take pictures of their own work areas and create a chart to display the photographs in a central place. They decide the dates for subsequent photography and set their own deadlines for improving the scene.

Pictures are taken whenever some countermeasure or improvement is implemented. The photographs are then displayed on a chart in time sequence, along with comments or evaluation points about the scenes.

Fixed-point photography displays effectively help people grasp the essence of a constantly changing situation. They provide unmistakable evidence of the results of improvement activities. These charts are like the satellite weather pictures on

Figure 3-2. The Main Elements of Fixed-point Photography

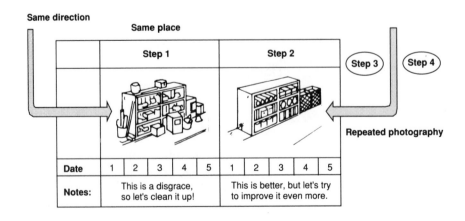

television. When you see how the picture changes from frame to frame, it is easier to understand what has taken place.

The display charts also provide an element of healthy embarrassment: they motivate employees to correct the problems in a specific area by the time the next "picture day" rolls around.

Fixed-point photography makes 5S improvements conspicuous even if this is the only measure taken. It helps to understand the psychological responses of people in the workplace:

- When people photograph their own weaknesses, they recognize their own shortcomings and become determined to improve the situation.
- Having pictures displayed in the center of the workplace is a lot more effective than hiding them away in a drawer. Workers cannot avoid seeing them, which encourages them to participate in improvement activities.
- People enjoy a sense of achievement and completion when the effects of their improvements are there for all to see.
- The photography charts tell an improvement story that becomes an excellent PR resource when dealing with clients, senior management, or others from outside the workplace.

Many companies have improved their performance by applying fixed-point photography throughout the company as a way to promote 5S activities.

Putting Things in Order

The first thing some people think of when they hear the words "putting things in order" (*seiri*), is "getting rid of something." Others protest that it is wasteful to throw things away; we should keep them.

This type of abstract debate confuses the true meaning of "putting in order," which is to sort and categorize things according to what is necessary and what is not. Then you can dispose of what you don't need. Among the things you do need, after careful consideration you will discover that you can further classify and arrange them in the best order for the work methods you are using. Some things need to be kept close at hand; things you use less frequently can be kept farther away. Figure 3-3 shows these interrelationships.

Proper Arrangement: The "Wide and Shallow" Rule

"Proper arrangement" (*seiton*) has to do with arranging things efficiently so that you can easily get to what you need and use things in the best order. This is especially important in storage situations. At a visit to a factory warehouse, I once saw steel pipes, wrapped in 50-pipe units, piled high on top of one another (see Figure 3-4). I was surprised to see this, so I asked the people there, "Well, how do you take out the pipes buried on the bottom?" They answered, "Oh, we get to them after the crane removes the ones piled on top."

While I was wondering whether the warehouse operators actually were skillful enough to move the top pipes with the

Figure 3-3. How to Promote Good Order

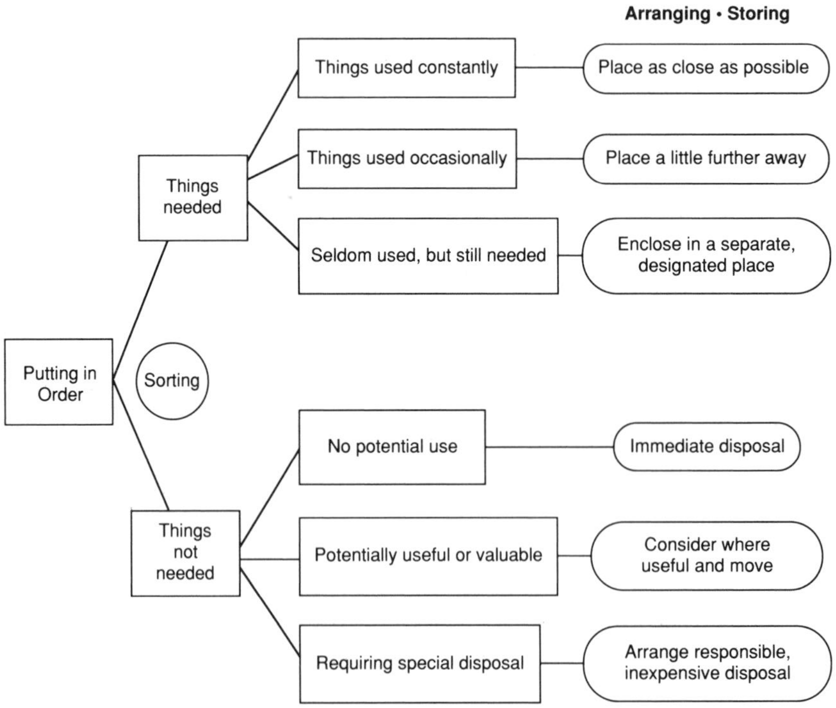

Figure 3-4. Proper Arrangement: Storage Examples

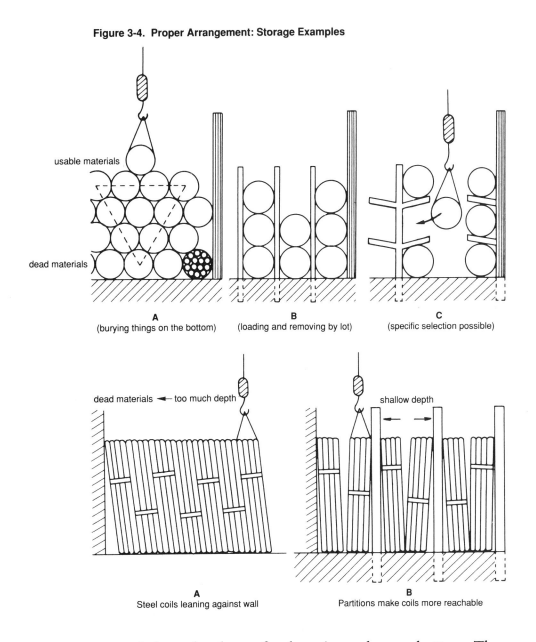

usable materials

dead materials

A
(burying things on the bottom)

B
(loading and removing by lot)

C
(specific selection possible)

dead materials ← too much depth

shallow depth

A
Steel coils leaning against wall

B
Partitions make coils more reachable

crane, I glanced at the tag for the units on the very bottom. They had been there for more than six months. The pipes looked rusty and corroded, and it was clear that it would be quite a while before the crane would get to them. This warehouse certainly wasn't set up to rotate the oldest inventory.

In order to make proper arrangement easy to understand, I like to compare an oblong storage chest with a chest of drawers. If you have an oblong chest, you can fill it up with anything, close the lid, and from the outside it will look nice and neat. But you won't be able to get to things at the bottom in a hurry. With a chest of drawers, however, it is as easy to take out what you want as it was to put it in, as long as you know where you put it.

The steel pipe storage situation was a lot like cramming things into a large oblong chest. To the extent that this irrationality remains, it will be almost impossible to have lot control, to say nothing of a common-sense, first-in, first-out approach. From a quality control perspective, this is one of the worst ways to manage inventory.

Therefore, I like to use the rule that proper arrangement involves a wide range, or a large number of ranges, as well as a shallow depth. A parking lot example will make this idea easily understood. Elevator-tower parking structures are used in some cities because they make efficient use of expensive real estate. They are relatively inconvenient to use, however, because they are "deep" — the first row of cars in is "parked in" by later arrivals — and have a "narrow" range — the elevator can park or retrieve only one car at a time. Sometimes they generate long waiting lines.

Street-level parking lots, by contrast, have a wide range — a car can drive to wherever there is an open spot — and a shallow depth — a car cannot be parked in. If this kind of parking lot is stacked to make a multilevel parking structure, it is possible to combine efficient land use with the freedom of individual cars to come and go. Figure 3-5 compares these different parking arrangements. The principles of efficient and convenient car "storage" apply as well to storage of parts, equipment, and finished goods.

Making It Easier to Maintain Order and Proper Arrangement

Examine your own work and storage areas. Look for problems with insufficient storage space, the way things are placed,

Figure 3-5. Comparison of Parking Layouts

Type	Description	Effective land use	Staffing problems	Pros and cons		Range	Depth
				Convenience	First-in, first-out		
A	Street-level lot	△	◎	○	◎	Wide (multiple spots)	Shallow (one car deep)
B	Multilevel drive-in structure	○	◎	○ Upper levels are inconvenient	◎	Wide	Shallow
C	Elevator tower structure	◎	△	△ Waiting lines	✕	Narrow (one car at a time)	Deep (double parking)

◎ = Very effective   △ = Problematic

○ = Somewhat effective   ✕ = Totally undesirable

Note: Exit booth location not considered

volume, and so on. You should be especially careful about how pallets are arranged or how goods or parts are loaded onto skids. When goods are lined up too deeply in large blocks, it is difficult to move things in and out and also costly due to factors such as forklift fuel costs and labor for loading, unloading, and restacking to reach the first-in (see Figures 3-6, 3-7, and 3-8).

Some tips on keeping things in order and properly arranged:

1. First, use the concept of "air-free engineering" to come up with ways to save space. In short, this means making new space by reorganizing things to eliminate wasted space. Doing this makes it easier to arrange things to keep them in order and to maintain clear aisles for traffic.

2. If aisles are maintained properly, things can be placed facing them. Try to avoid placing things in areas that don't face the aisles — it will take more time to retrieve them and make it impossible to maintain a system of first-in, first-out storage.

3. Whenever possible, store things in a shallow layout. If it is impossible to avoid a deep layout, use roller conveyors to

Figure 3-6. Wide Range and Shallow Depth

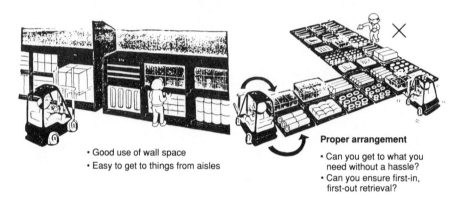

- Good use of wall space
- Easy to get to things from aisles

Proper arrangement

- Can you get to what you need without a hassle?
- Can you ensure first-in, first-out retrieval?

Figure 3-7. Arranging Pallets

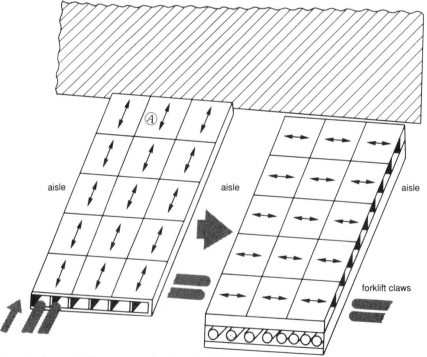

Lay out pallets so forklift can remove them from the aisles

move the goods, and control traffic with separate entrances and exits.

4. When placing things facing the aisle, avoid stacking the containers so the tops ones must be removed to get to the lower ones. Whenever possible, use racks or pallets for each item.

5. Do not make aisles directly beside windows. In windowed areas, the support posts usually project from the walls, resulting in dead space. Turn this area into useful space by storing a single row of dollies or pallets there or putting jigs and tools there on low shelves.

6. Areas, lot numbers, and designated goods should all be clearly labeled in the storage area. Anyone should be able to understand the situation at a glance (see Figures 3-9 and 3-10).

7. For tools, measuring devices, and other equipment used for die changeovers, set out only the minimum number required. One efficient way to do this is to prepare a cart that is ready to go with all the necessary elements for a changeover — and nothing else.

Cleaning Is More Than Skin Deep

"Cleaning" (*seisō*) means preventing any surface in the workplace from remaining dirty or soiled and using machinery and equipment to keep everything sparkling so the workplace stays in a smoothly running condition. Although no other concept is as important, there is no other word with as many different interpretations. One generally accepted idea is that "cleaning" is just a matter of sweeping up and keeping any dirt from being seen. But the workplace needs more than just a superficial brush-up.

I once visited a factory that produces electronic components. Extremely clean manufacturing conditions are vital to the quality of the final product of this company. In a room near the plant entrance, people who enter are vacuumed to remove dust from their clothing and body. People then put on surgical caps and gowns and replace their street shoes with slippers. While I was admiring the factory's cleanliness policy and staring intently at the production line, I noticed something that surprised me.

Figure 3-8. Poor Bin Arrangement

Parts on the bottom can't be reached without moving bins on top

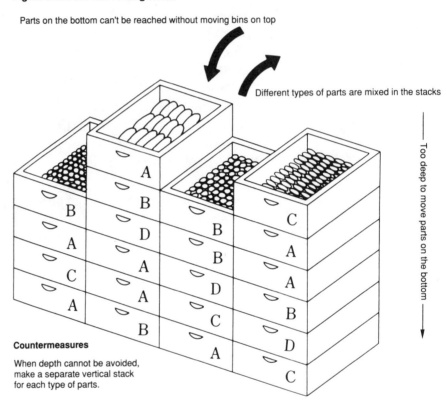

Different types of parts are mixed in the stacks

Too deep to move parts on the bottom →

Countermeasures

When depth cannot be avoided, make a separate vertical stack for each type of parts.

Figure 3-9. Storing Jigs and Dies

Use labels for specific items

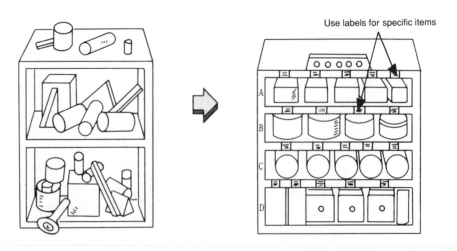

Figure 3-10. Storing Tools and Gages

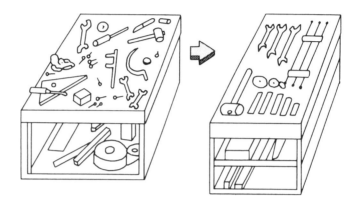

On the lampshade for the fluorescent light over one work-bench, there was a thick layer of dust — so much that you could write in it with your finger. A lot of dust had also settled on the blower of the air conditioner, with no sign of any cleaning having been done there. At this point, it was obvious that there was some misunderstanding about the meaning of "cleaning."

If you hear a crunch when people walk on the floor and it is covered with oil stains and metal chips, the factory is not clean. Is the glass on the machine gauge so cloudy that you can't even see the position of the needle? Perhaps you have an operations standards manual, but it sits on the shelf because it is impossible to read yellowed pages covered with grease marks. Or maybe your factory's "maintenance program" consists of periodic lubrication and bolt tightening.

The fix-up efforts made in most workplaces are not adequate to merit the label of "cleaning." Real cleaning is something that comes from the heart, reflecting pride in the workplace — even a kind of affection. The spirit of the word "cleaning" implies *polishing things beautifully*, not just sweeping up a little bit. The halls of a Buddhist temple shine because the monks who live there clean and polish them. Real cleaning requires this kind of dedication.

As you clean and polish, you can start to detect oil and air leaks as well as defective parts or abnormal operations. This is known as a "cleaning inspection," or looking for problems as you take care of the machines and work area. The steps in a cleaning inspection include

- Sweeping with a broom
- Wiping
- Inspecting
- Polishing
- Painting
- Maintaining cleanliness

The Meaning of "Purity"

"Purity" (*seiketsu*) means removing germs and stains as well as maintaining a situation of cleanliness. Cleaning and maintaining purity are actually inseparable: implementing one means implementing the other. Purity is especially significant for work with food products, pharmaceutical products, biotechnology, and electronic components.

At Honda Motor Company, workers have worn white uniforms since the company was founded. The idea behind this was that since dirt stands out on white, uniforms can be cleaned immediately, and cleanliness can be maintained. Although this famous idea came from the company's founder, Soichiro Honda, a company needs original ideas like this from all its employees to develop a consensus on the value of maintaining purity in the workplace.

Commitment: The Key Factor

Ultimately, the 4S principles — putting in order, proper arrangement, cleaning, and purity — have value in the workplace only when the employees are committed to following them. It is important for people to grasp the essence of these principles and to care enough to actually carry them out on the job.

Back in 1955 Yamaha Motor became independent from its parent company, Nippon Gakki, and began operating with only a hundred or so employees in a factory that was little more than a shack. The first things employees received when they joined the company were time cards and *zori*, simple Japanese sandals that were traditionally worn at home instead of shoes. The president, Gen'ichi Kawakami, gave the following words to the surprised recruits: "We are a small company and our buildings are old, but I hope that everyone will try hard to make this a first-rate factory. *Treat your factory as if it were the best guest room in your own home.* Please wear these company 'house slippers' to remind you of this." *

Our factory building was a humble frame building put up during the war. We painted the outside and planted a lawn around it, which was quite unusual for that time. Since we didn't have much money, we covered the interior with simple white tempera paint from the crossbeams to the floor, making a bright and cheerful atmosphere.

The floors were regarded as though they belonged in the guestroom of a private home, so they were swept thoroughly, all the way to the concrete edges. If the slightest crunch was heard underfoot, we immediately cleaned them again.

Once the president was making the rounds on a factory inspection. Someone pointed out an oil leak in the five-ton hydraulic press in the engine assembly section that I managed. I mumbled a lame excuse to him, saying that we had previously requested the machine maintenance section to fix it, but it had not yet been repaired.

The president would hear nothing of it. "You cannot excuse yourself simply by saying you put in a maintenance request. The oil is still leaking, isn't it? If no one comes to fix it, then *you*, the production section manager, should fix it! You can ask your staff people to help you, but don't take people off the line to manage your own responsibility!"

---

* Other companies in Japan also use the concept of the "parlor factory" to keep the work environment immaculately clean. Seiichi Nakajima's book, *Introduction to TPM* (Productivity Press, 1988), describes Aishin Seiki's Nishio pump factory, where workers also remove their shoes at the door. — Ed.

Three hours after this reprimand, we managed to finish repairing the leak by ourselves. This incident led me to make a personal commitment to lead my employees in getting the workplace cleaned up and keeping it that way. As president Kawakami pointed out, this is management's responsibility. His commitment required us to go beyond blame and excuses and to actually do the work.

This was how things went for the first several years at Yamaha Motor. President Kawakami taught us directly how managers ought to lead their workers, beginning with 5S. This kind of discipline developed a commitment to adhering to these basic principles at the management, supervisor, and operator levels.

To summarize, I would like to share some observations gleaned from my experience in managing 5S programs:

- In a *third-rate workplace* people leave trash, and no one stops to picks it up.
- In a *second-rate workplace* people leave trash, but others pick it up.
- In a *first-rate workplace* no one leaves trash, but people would pick it up if they saw it.

CHAPTER 4

Observing and Writing: An Introduction to the Big 3 Memo

The Importance of Careful Observation

Whenever we want to improve something, we begin with observation. The essence of observation is stopping other activities and watching. You have to stand still for a moment and look at things carefully, without becoming distracted. In the workplace this means spending five minutes intently scrutinizing one particular area or process. Five minutes is less than 1 percent of the 480 minutes in an eight-hour day.

Try viewing a particular area through a paper tube. This little exercise helps focus attention and make things more visible to observers. It is amazing how it reveals things that people never noticed before!

For effective observation, you need a framework. The problem-free engineering method combines the three basic problems of irrationality, inconsistency, and waste with the 5W1H method mentioned in Chapter 2. Look for points that can be improved. You should come up with questions like "Why does this job take so much walking?" or "Why does it involve so much waiting time?"

Next, apply 5W1H, asking "what, why, where, when, who, and how" to gather more information about the situation. Asking these questions helps make the problems of irrationality, inconsistency, and waste more concrete. For example:

Q: What am I doing?
A: Sorting things out.
Q: Why do I have to do it?
A: Because there are defectives mixed in with good ones.
Q: Where did the defects come from?
A: From Process 398.
Q: Who is the operator there?
A: Chuck W.
Q: When did you first notice that defectives were included?
A: A check yesterday showed an unusually high defect rate.
Q: How can the defects be prevented?
A: We need some kind of source inspection for the preceding process.

After you have observed and collected information about the situation, then write a memo to record the problem.

Making a Note of It

The word *nekanben* means an idea that comes to a person while he or she is resting or sleeping. Many people experience such a flash of insight at night while their minds are relaxed. When they wake up the next morning, though, the brilliant idea has vanished.

The late Kaichi Kawakami, former president of Nippon Gakki, recommended keeping a notepad under the pillow so that good ideas that occur in the middle of the night can be jotted down. If you don't make a note, you may lose a precious insight before you can put it to use.

Recording your observations is very important. Once people learn the problem-free engineering approach, they should jot down memos about their situations, even when no improvement ideas immediately come to mind. Whether it's just a passing thought or a problem point that has taken a lot of effort to grasp, the idea will soon evaporate if it isn't written down.

To highlight "Invention Month" activities in Japan, a television program presented a panel of senior production workers who talked about innovations and good ideas. The moderator asked them how they came up with creative ideas to help their jobs. The participants responded unanimously that while they went about their daily work, they always used memos to jot down anything they found frustrating, difficult, or inconvenient to do or anything else they noticed. All felt that this was an essential part of their jobs. They were always thinking about how to solve the problems they noted in their memos and asking themselves, "Isn't there some way to better deal with this?"

Some people hold that taking notes in meetings or presentations keeps them from listening attentively to what is being said, and extremely intelligent people with extraordinary memory power probably do not need written reminders. But those of us with imperfect memories will benefit from keeping a Big 3 Memo workbook and jotting things down constantly. It is the best start on the road to problem solving — a path that winds through mountains of daily problems but can lead to copper or silver or even gold.

Two Strategies for Workplace Improvement

All improvement activities have two basic parts: detecting problems and solving them. Problem detection includes getting a basic understanding of problems and their causes. Some types of problems must be studied carefully in order to eventually solve them. To do this, analyze the problem using the most effective methods possible, including industrial engineering and quality control techniques. I refer to this way of attacking problems as "strategy A."

As Figure 4-1 shows, progress in strategy A involves

- Selecting an improvement theme
- Observing and collecting data
- Examining the data
- Doing further research if necessary
- Creating several alternative proposals
- Evaluating the effectiveness of these proposals
- Drawing up evaluation, selection, and implementation plans

When an improvement proposal is established or implemented, it is recorded on a Big 3 Memo. Ultimately, the goal is to create a new, improved standard for the situation.

Many problems, however, do not require this much analysis and effort to understand and solve. Problems identified with the problem-free engineering approach often can be solved with fewer steps. I call this shortcut "strategy B." Consider this example of how it works:

- Observe the workplace with "walk-free" (detecting unnecessary walking) in mind.
- Immediately record problem points on the top part of a Big 3 Memo.
- Change the location.
- Make a "walk-free" workplace.

As this example shows, it is often possible to improve things quickly, without a lot of analysis. You can note the gain in effi-

Figure 4-1. Problem-solving with Strategies A and B

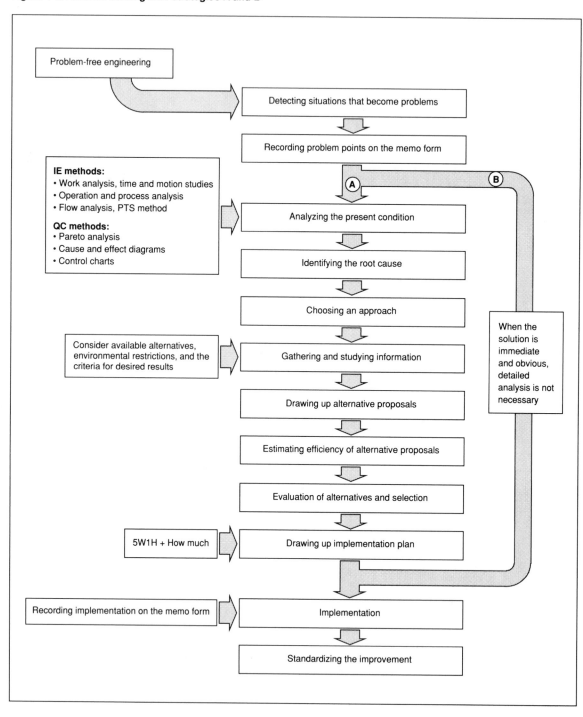

ciency by recording some figures on cost-saving in the lower part of the memo form. For many problems, using strategy A to analyze the problem and evaluate different solutions can sometimes waste a lot of effort without significantly improving the efficiency of the situation. Using strategy B and recording simple ideas on the Big 3 Memo, small efforts can show some results, which makes people feel good about their involvement in the improvement process.

A flexible approach to problem solving uses strategies A and B as required by the problem. Many of the improvement examples shown in this book were in fact developed using strategy B.

When you set out to achieve improvement, you don't necessarily have to make a frontal attack with all of your resources; you can also sneak up from behind for a quick strike. You have to know when you need all the analysis of strategy A and when a simpler method will work just as well. The best way to root out waste is to learn to use both methods appropriately.

Using the Big 3 Memo

The Big 3 Memo is a tool for detecting irrationality, inconsistency, and waste in the workplace and for understanding the situation. People can strengthen their powers of perception and insight and learn to observe their own worksites very carefully. As they do this, they record their observations for future reference in making improvements. Some points on how to use the Big 3 Memo follow:

- It is helpful to keep a memo workbook handy for jotting down your observations.
- Whenever you notice a problem point (irrationality, inconsistency, or waste), record it directly on a Big 3 Memo form.
- Even when an improvement idea does not immediately come to mind, get into the habit of jotting down the problems on the top part of the memo form. A drawing of the situation will help clarify the situation.
- When a solution is devised, write it on the bottom part of the form, along with a drawing of the changes you propose.

- Calculate the benefits of the improvement, if possible, in terms of money saved.
- Submit the completed memo for whatever approvals may be required.
- Save time in submitting proposals to the suggestion system by attaching a photocopy of the completed memo to a suggestion form.

Although it was developed in manufacturing plants, the Big 3 Memo system can be used for activities to improve office organization, delivery of services, and other nonindustrial situations. The Big 3 Memo can be used by individuals as well as small groups. The collected information can be used "horizontally" by other groups to expand know-how throughout the company. Figure 4-2 provides an overview of an improvement system that incorporates the Big 3 Memo.

Contents of the Big 3 Memo Workbook

The Big 3 Memo workbook keeps memos in one place and offers useful information about the improvement process. It includes the following sections:

- A checklist of workplace improvement expectations
- Four Ways to Improve the Workplace
- Big 3 Memo log sheets
- Hints for using the Big 3 Memo
- Applying the principles of motion economy
- The Big 3 Memo matrix
- Ten guidelines for effective use of the Big 3 Memo
- Problem-free engineering by factory management area
- How to promote improvements with the Big 3 Memo program
- Big 3 Memo forms

A sample Big 3 Memo workbook is included at the end of this book.★

★ Offprints of the workbook are available from Productivity Press. — Ed.

Figure 4-2. An Improvement System Using the Big 3 Memo

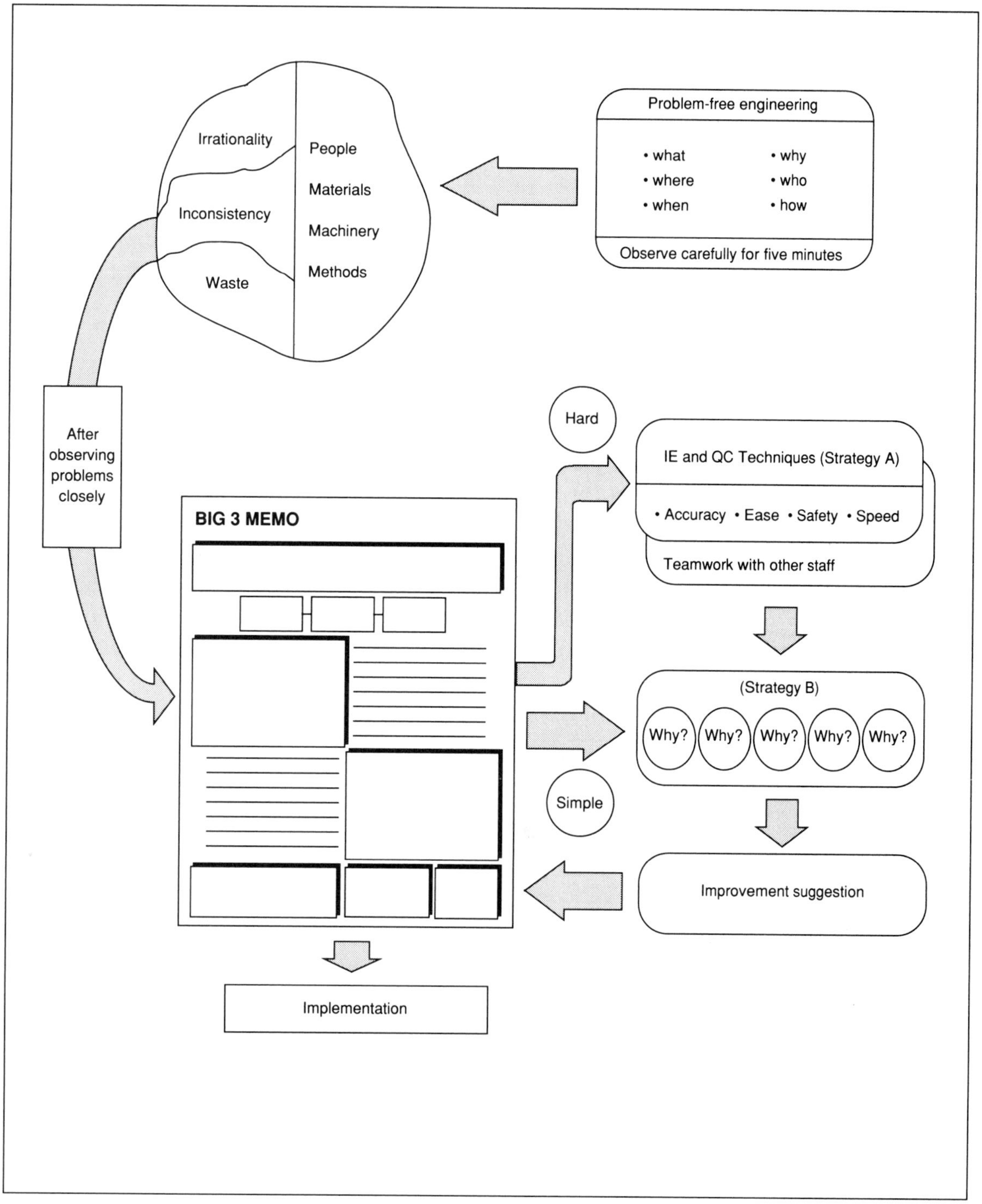

Irrationality

People

Inconsistency

Materials

Machinery

Waste

Methods

Problem-free engineering

- what
- why
- where
- who
- when
- how

Observe carefully for five minutes

After observing problems closely

Hard

IE and QC Techniques (Strategy A)

- Accuracy • Ease • Safety • Speed

Teamwork with other staff

BIG 3 MEMO

(Strategy B)

Why? Why? Why? Why? Why?

Simple

Improvement suggestion

Implementation

How to Fill Out the Big 3 Memo

Figure 4–3 points out the various parts of the memo form. When writing up a memo, don't forget to fill in the spaces for dates, write down the problem points in order, use 5W1H to understand the situation, and develop a quantitative grasp of the problem. These points help simplify calculations of cost savings or improvement in efficiency. See Chapter 7 for examples of completed memo forms for many types of problem-free engineering.

Recording Efficiency and Cost Savings

Figure 4–4 shows the workbook's log form for recording the memos as they are begun and tallying the increase in efficiency resulting from improvements. It works something like a deposit passbook for problem point data banks. The employee makes entries under the appropriate headings for completed improvements, incomplete situations, costs saved per month, and a cumulative total of savings from the combined improvements.

In many companies, supervisors use the "Comments" column to sign off with initials, date, and notes about the problem or idea. By making these entries, workers and supervisors keep a clear idea of progress made on improving various observed situations and the total cost savings resulting from improvements.

Figure 4-3. The Parts of a Big 3 Memo form

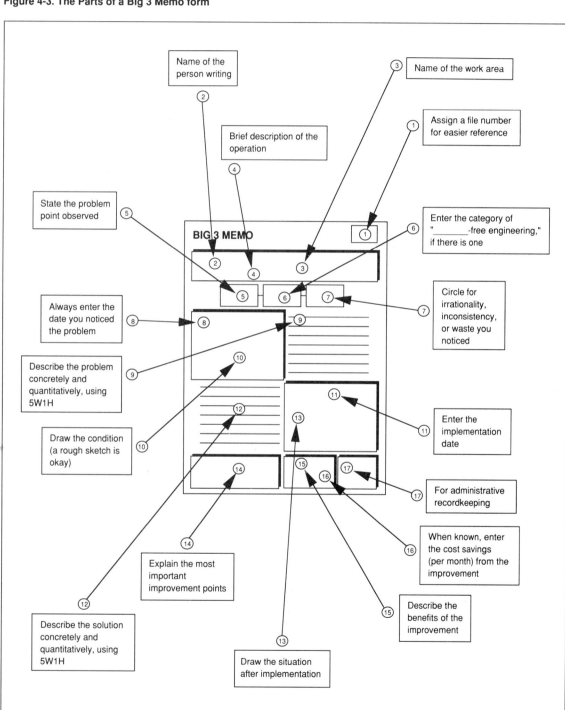

Figure 4-4. Big 3 Memo Log Sheet

This page serves as a log of the contents of an employee's Big 3 Memo form notebook as well as a record of the cost savings from implemented improvements. The writer makes an entry here whenever he or she writes a memo.

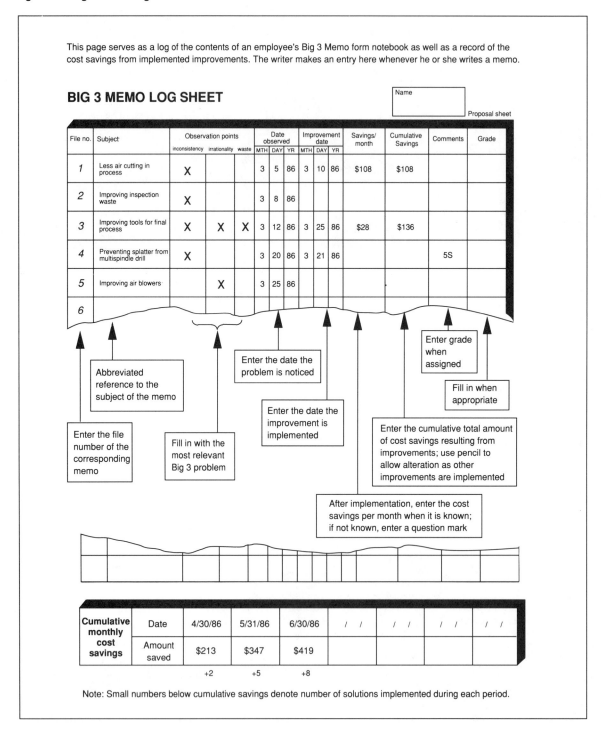

CHAPTER 5

Ten Guidelines for Effective Use of the Big 3 Memo

1. For Managers: Use the Memo to Manage Details

Modern managers have to work long hours at a hectic pace. They carrying responsibility for P (productivity), Q (quality), C (cost), D (delivery), S (safety), and M (morale), which leaves them in a state of constant physical and mental fatigue. In this condition, it is easy to forget about problems that could be improved. The Big 3 Memo is a good way for busy people to remember important ideas.

Shuji Kikuyama, section chief of the base metal quality control section at Yamaha, is an enthusiastic leader in management use of the memo. When he writes down customers' concerns and complaints on a memo form in their presence, his commitment to do something about their problems is recognized. Figure 5-1 shows an example of his memos.

When such a simple exercise can win the trust of the company's customers, it should not be ignored. I recommend the memo as a method that can help any manager handle the details of his or her responsibilities more effectively.

2. For Supervisors: Use the Memo to Lead Improvement Activities

People in supervisory positions have to master five basic areas of knowledge or skill:

Knowledge of the work

It is important to understand the technologies and skills required for each worker's job, including materials, machines, tools, processes, operating methods, and engineering.

Knowledge of responsibilities

A supervisor must know how to do the work in accordance with company policy, contracts and agreements, rules, safety regulations, administrative reporting, and production plans.

Figure 5-1. A Manager's Big 3 Memo

BIG 3 MEMO

Plant: Kotobuki Kinzoku Kogyo, Ltd., Seki Factory

File No.	19
8/85	

Name: Shuji Kikuyama	Section:	Worksite:	Group:

Machine Type: 15111-1470	Line/Parts: Oil pump pressure leak	Process: in-house casting

Observation Points:

┌─ Point ─┐	┌─ -free Engineering ─┐	┌─ Big 3 Problem ─┐
2 skills	Failure-free	Irrationality Inconsistency (Waste)

Present Condition

August 28, 1985

Defects:

date	in-house	vendor
8/7	39	40
8/9	47	27
8/19	27	35
8/20	72	38
8/21	64	0
8/22	74	0
8/26	115	15
8/27	138	13
8/28	13	
8/29	15	

Approximate area of pressure leak

Observation:

#2 Because of a pressure leak in the 15111-1470 oil pump, it was replaced with a new one from the warehouse, but there were still many defects every day.

• 15-20% defects

• Line is dangerous

Countermeasure: Use color-check powder to check inventory for blowhole defects. Consider deploying ASAP.

After Improvements:

Temporary countermeasure: Carefully check finished product. Approx. 3000 items Completed 9/3
Long-term countermeasure: Repair die, then perform air pressure test. To eliminate the defects, round off places that are angled, so that blowholes will be reduced.

Test items: 100, on 8/30
Results: 0/100 = no defects

Note: Defects will increase as the die ages, but adjustments can prevent this to some extent.

After Improvement

August 29, 1985

(adjusting and rounding off)

Improvement Points

Results

Cost Savings/Gain:

Suggestion No.

suggested under name of Mr. Tasaka

Grade: completed

Job instruction skill

When employees are well trained and have the skills they need to make excellent products or give quality service, they can avoid defects, accidents, and quality complaints from the customers. This can help to improve productivity and customer relations.

Leadership skills

A supervisor must know how to foster cooperation among employees and be able to help their working relationships progress smoothly. He or she must find ways to recognize subordinates for their effort and participation, and to remind them that they are the strength behind any workplace improvement effort.

Skill in improving job methods

To make improvements, you have to break down operations into their basic elements and study them in detail. This book emphasizes such skills as simplifying things, deciding the best sequence, and then combining the ideas to eliminate unnecessary things.

Supervisors, of course, are just as busy as managers; it is no easy matter for them to polish all of these skills and areas of knowledge. Possibly because improvement efforts take a back seat to actual problems for which they are accountable, such as poor quality or an accident, supervisors' skills in improvement methods probably vary the most widely. It is nevertheless important to make the effort and not just coast between problems.

Supervisors are leaders of people. Their job is to ensure quality and improvement, regardless of whether they themselves make an improvement in the literal sense of the word. They need skill in problem detecting and solving to help workers learn how to make improvements of their own. Their direct support of workers is indispensable.

I recommend the Big 3 Memo as something to help supervisors continually observe the workplace and keep track of problems that arise. If the supervisor isn't able to follow through on an improvement after noting a problem on the memo form, he or she can ask other staff members to help do something about it.

The memo supports the daily effort of keeping the improvement process alive in the workplace.

---

3. For Hourly Employees: Use the Memo as a Way to Participate

How can a company encourage its operating-level employees to make improvement suggestions? Company management and small group activity leaders have to address this question, whether they like it or not. Trying to force things to happen from the top down, using pressure and ordering people to do things, is generally ineffective and understandably leads to negative attitudes among the work force. A better approach heightens awareness of the importance of making improvement proposals.

To Encourage Employees to Become Active Workers

When you try to make a person who doesn't want to do something do it anyway, you are applying force, possibly without realizing it. If you are a manager or supervisor, this thought should scare you a little.

Let's consider the matter. How would you feel if you worked at the same station all day, every day, and were expected simply to do whatever work your supervisor gave you, without questions? The job may be beyond your skill level, or perhaps you notice a problem that needs attention, but in many cases you might as well have your mouth taped shut. You have no opportunity to describe the way the job is being done or to use your creativity to find ways to do it better.

An employee in this situation feels he or she is only a step or two above an ox turning circles around a stone mill. But workers are human beings, and the greatest attribute of our humanness is the ability to think. That is why it is important to be able to make improvement suggestions: It is simply a way to exercise your unique human creativity.

When workers understand and adopt this attitude, they will change from passive employees into active workers. A problem-free engineering program using the Big 3 Memo provides the opportunity to participate in how things are done in the workplace. Success of the program is measured by the extent to which people become aware they have something to contribute. As this happens, they stop feeling like the ox grinding the grain. They come to feel that their improvement suggestions are expressions they are making for themselves and not just because the company asks them to.

To Encourage Solutions

No matter how hard we try to think of improvement ideas, it is not easy to come up with solutions. In fact, sometimes thinking really hard to come up with a good solution to a problem has the opposite result — ideas seem to elude us. Good ideas for solutions begin with detecting problems and making memos about them. The Big 3 Memo has a proven track record for producing solutions to workplace problems.

Figure 5-2 shows the results of an eight-month survey made during fiscal 1987 at companies using the Big 3 Memo throughout the entire company. This survey focused on the number of days elapsed from the time the problem was detected and noted on the memo form until the time improvement suggestions were made to deal with them. Results of the survey indicated that it can take several weeks, or occasionally months, for solutions to be devised and improvement suggestions made. It is a good idea, therefore, to keep the observation and problem-detection process going on a regular basis.

This kind of survey and graph are good ways to show everyone in the company the results they have produced and keep people interested in the effect of their efforts.

4. Find and Solve Problems at Their Source

It is no easy task to track down criminals once you have lost sight of them. It takes the combined efforts of many people and a tremendous amount of energy to catch them. The more time it takes, the smaller the chance of success.

Similarly, at a production site, it's no problem if the cause of a quality defect can be located on the same day it occurs. But by

Figure 5-2. Problem Detection and Number of Days Required Until Solution

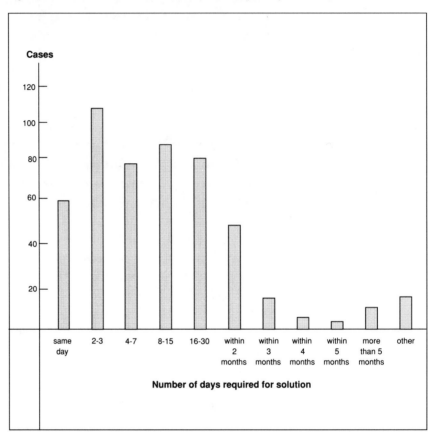

the time we get around to analysis or data studies to retrace what happened, it is too late.

Quality — or a defect — is created by the process. Quality control, then, ultimately amounts to control at the source. This means immediately going for a hard look at the actual state of the actual site of the problem. Whenever you detect a problem or defect, immediately record the relevant facts on the Big 3 Memo form. This creates a problem investigation notebook.

Figure 5–3 shows an example of a memo used to record a problem detected on the spot. The five-minute observation focused on the water that trickles down on the edge of the doctor blade to prevent dirt and lint from sticking to the roller of the paper manufacturing machine. Now and then the roller rotated more slowly. When this happened, the employee noticed, the water fell down in drops on the rolled paper instead of being distributed evenly by the doctor. This caused tears and defective paper, which were detected at the source of the problem.

Improvement suggestions were then considered. Five days later, the doctor blade position was changed slightly so that it contacted the roller at a different place. This created a small dam, which prevented the water from overflowing even when the roller speed varied. Using the Big 3 Memo, the problem was corrected at the source, resulting in zero defects.

5. Use the Memo Method as a Preventive Measure

I pointed out how much more effective it is to apprehend criminals at the scene of the crime than to try to catch them after they get away. The crime has still occurred, however, and in some cases has done a lot of damage. Wouldn't it be better to find a way to prevent the crime from taking place — to prevent criminals from developing?

In the workplace, too, it's better to prevent defects in the first place than to correct a problem that has already developed. This means hands-on management right from the start, to deal with anything relevant to quality. It means using poka-yoke (mistake-proofing) devices skillfully to catch defects at the source. In safety matters, it means training supervisors and operators in safe operating methods and accident prevention techniques.

The ideal situation is detecting and solving problems, at the source whenever possible, after five minutes of careful observation. Many times you won't notice any particular abnormality. There may still be things you can do, however, to prevent future mishaps. To develop these preventive methods, use hypothetical questions to consider various factors that could result in defects or accidents. Ask "What if this were the case?" "How can

Figure 5-3. Using the Big 3 Memo to Solve Problems at the Source

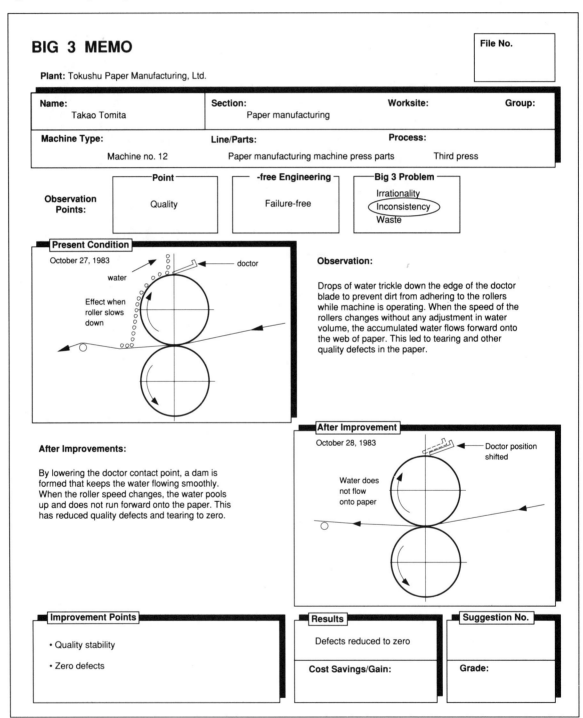

we make this area 'slip-free' or 'pinch-free'?" You may detect some surprising things with this approach (see Figure 5- 4).

After participating in one of my seminars, a section chief from one company related a personal story. "I followed your suggestion of observing the job carefully three times, but I couldn't find any problem. I was impatient and wanted to quit before spending even five minutes on it. Then I gave it one more look from a slightly different perspective, remembering a major accident that had recently occurred at the company. This time, I noticed something that surprised me! A potential problem occurred to me that reminded me of the accident situation. So I wrote it down right away in my Big 3 Memo. The importance of your advice to take the full five minutes for observation really came home to me."

6. Record Cost Savings Information with the Memo

When calculating the factory manager's annual statement one year, I reached final figures that showed factory profits were greater than had been estimated. I believed that this was because some benefits, especially improvement results from the first-line supervisors, simply did not show up on the asset side in the estimate.

Although it is often impractical for supervisors in many Japanese companies to directly make improvement suggestions, they are in fact responsible for many improvements, either their own or their subordinates, that benefit the company. Their contribution is important and ought to be included as part of the entire company's savings from the improvement suggestion system. My search for a method to collect information that shows this contribution was primarily responsible for the concept of the Big 3 Memo system.

Calculating total amounts saved is easy because all employees use the same tools — a Big 3 Memo workbook with log sheets, and the type of company costing sheet shown in Figure A-9. Employees and supervisors figure the savings on each memo form and keep track of savings on the log sheets. Here are two examples showing the effectiveness of calculating techniques.

Figure 5-4. Relationships Between Solving Problems at the Source and Preventing Mishaps

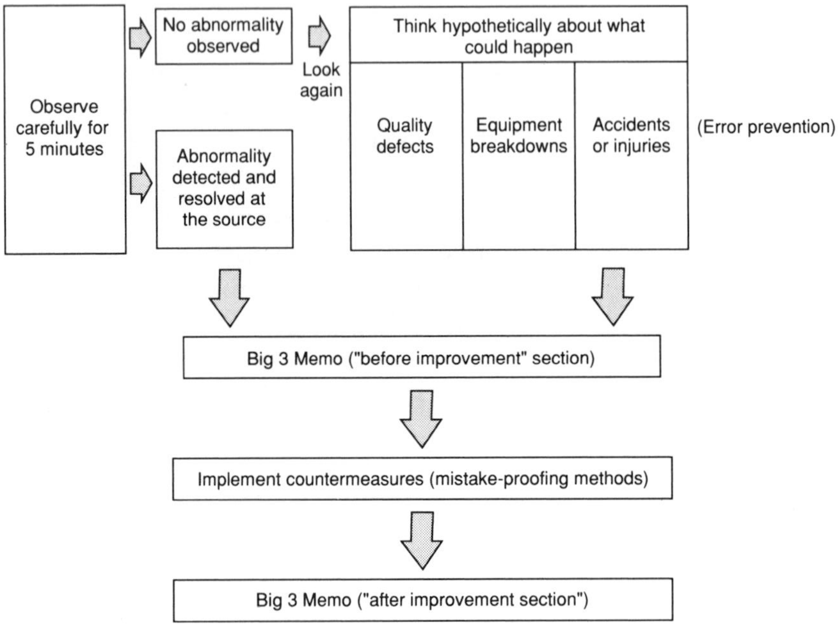

Example 1

In spring 1984 I received the following letter from Yoshiaki Matsuo, then foreman of a machine shop in one of the Yamaha Motor production sections:

☞ *We would like to inform you that our section has introduced a Total Productive Maintenance (TPM) program in which all employees participate and that we are now making progress toward achieving our goal of raising productivity. While conducting this program and relying heavily on the guidebook for the Big 3 Memo, we have achieved impressive results that we never imagined possible. One of the ways the guidebook suggests using the memo to promote improvement activities is as "a standard that first-line supervisors can use to gauge their own performance in promoting improvement activities and getting people in the habit of doing them."*

When I read that, I just accepted it at face value and carried out Big 3 Memo activities accordingly. Now, when I review the records I kept in the log, I am surprised to see that we came up with 569 problem points during the period from January 1979, when we began, to November 1983.

During the time we were dealing with those 569 problems, there were many times when I thought to myself, "Let's call it a day and do it tomorrow." But I kept on going and pushed myself hard with thoughts like "If you don't do it today, you won't get into the habit of using the memo, but if you do use it regularly, the job will be a lot easier to do." When I use a memo form, I can take a long, hard, objective look at myself regardless of how busy I am. The important point, therefore, is that while I focus on problems that occur in the workplace, I have come to believe in my ability to deal with them effectively.

I think that using staff members effectively is another sign of a supervisor's skill. To deploy people effectively, supervisors make hard decisions about such things as the relative difficulty and priority of importance of various problems, carefully assessing the situations that turn up in the Big 3 Memo. We were able to conduct very efficient improvement operations to solve these problems, with a high degree of understanding and compliance among our staff members. Having the memo as a tool and guide certainly contributed to the smooth, cooperative problem-solving efforts of the staff. This is one of the most significant benefits of using the Big 3 Memo.

Our responsibility as supervisors regarding any one of these points is to determine how to reflect this desire for improvement in our daily work and then to implement what we have learned. I believe that by constantly broadening the scope for using the Big 3 Memo and getting into the habit of using it regularly, we are taking advantage of a shortcut on the way to rebuilding our companies.

Mr. Matsuo included one of his log sheets to show how he regularly recorded each problem point day by day. His boss, Mr. Kinoshita, also signed off on each point every day. This foreman's hard work and his boss's attention to these matters obviously paid off.

Example 2

Foreman Rokuro Mushu, who worked with a production section at the Yamaha Motor Hamakita factory, used the Big 3

Memo for six years to direct twenty or so subordinates in improvement activities. At the 1987 First-line Supervisors Convention, sponsored by the Japan Management Association, Mr. Mushu caused a stir with a paper on calculating the cost savings that had been carefully recorded in memos. Figure 5-5 shows some of the statistics for the six-year period. The total savings per month from these improvements was an impressive ¥12,697,000 ($50,500) in 1985 (a projected annual total of ¥152,364,000 ($606,000)). Figure 5-6, Completed Units per Person, and Figure 5-7, Percentage of Units Completed without Breakdowns, show results that greatly exceeded the target.

Anyone can achieve extraordinary results now and then. But keeping up this level of activity over six years requires great persistence and commitment.

I was the general manager of production at the time this program first started up. Foreman Mushu came to see me during those early days and told me he was not all that enthusiastic about the time and effort it would take to use the Big 3 Memo system. I pointed out to him that as a leader of other people his own involvement was vital to getting employees involved in making improvements. I reminded him, "A broken drum makes no sound."

Foreman Mushu did not want to be a "broken drum" of a leader and vowed that some day he would get me to recognize his work. His six years of effort deserve great credit.

---

7. Promote a Cooperative Improvement Strategy for Line Workers and Staff

One vivid memory I have from my time as head of a production section at Yamaha is how bad we felt when people from outside the section pointed out our problems to us. When the problems were things I myself had already noticed, others' criticism was easier to take. On the other hand, when outsiders saw things I didn't know about, it made me defensive — I tried to deny there was any reasonable basis for the criticism.

Figure 5-5. Yamaha Motor Production Section 1: Big 3 Memo Monthly Performance Graph

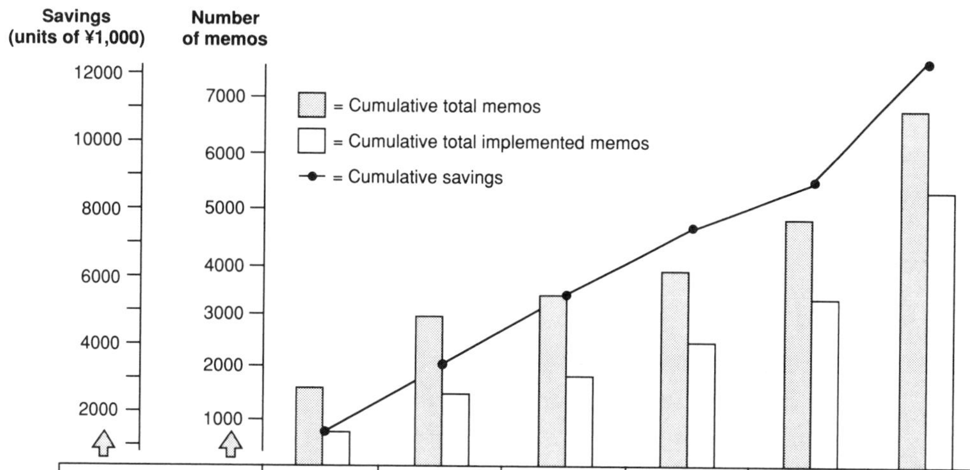

Cost savings figures (monthly average /cumulative)	1981	1982	1983	1984	1985	1986
Memo entries	1509/	1298/2807	550/3357	751/4108	804/4912	2088/7000
Implemented memos	678/	827/1505	435/1940	552/2492	621/3113	1626/4739
Cost savings	1211/	2206/3417	2044/5461	1849/7310	1459/8769	3928/12697

1985 savings: ¥12,697,000 ($50,500)/month (est. ¥152,364,000 ($606,000)/year)

Figure 5-6. Completed Units per Person

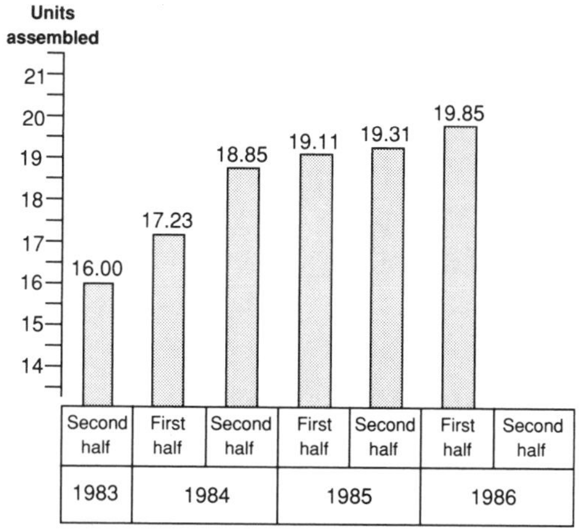

Figure 5-7. Percentage of Units Completed without Breakdowns

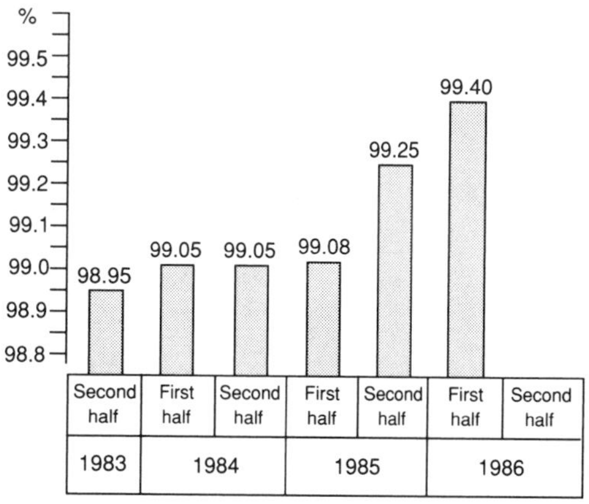

Others shared this kind of attitude, and it was responsible for frequent confrontations, some more serious than others, between line workers and supervisors and the engineering and maintenance staff people. This problem could not be solved easily because it was not a matter of reason or logic but of emotion.

One manifestation of this problem was that line supervisors were not enthusiastic about improvement projects that technical staff people came in to direct. They had no sense of being entrusted with responsibility for carrying out these projects. There was no sense of mission.

Line supervisors should never be in a situation where they feel they are merely executing proposals endorsed by the technical staff, under pressure from their supervisors. This almost ensures many failed improvement efforts. From beginning to end, workers and supervisors will complain that they can't agree completely with the proposal — they can't buy in to something they had no part in developing.

Problem solving is the responsibility of every person in the workplace. Operators have a lot of knowledge about the workplace situation, but without problem-solving skills and a method to express them, they can only struggle with technical staff people about how to make improvements. Problem-solving skills should be nurtured throughout the company. Constantly evaluating one's own work area is one way to build these skills. The Big 3 Memo is a good tool for helping hourly workers develop this awareness.

Solving the problems that are identified is sometimes simple and sometimes not. Figure 5-8 shows a typical relationship between the number of problems identified and the number of solutions implemented. Even if a problem is identified early, solutions are implemented for only 30 to 50 percent of them during the month. And it is practically certain that some problems will remain unsolved for a very long time.

As a former foreman, I believe that supervisors and line workers should not ignore this gap simply because some problems are more difficult to fix. These are situations we want to resolve, and if our own skills and knowledge are not adequate, we should ask the technical staff to assist us.

Figure 5-8. Gap Between Problems Detected and Problems Solved

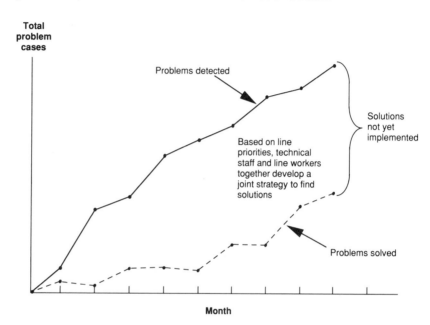

Staff members are generally hard-working people who are always increasing their specialized knowledge. It is their job to respond when there is an opportunity to help line workers. They are like the prompters that help actors and actresses get through difficult parts of the script. Both roles are important, and the staff and line workers should learn to see that they are working for a common purpose.

Therefore, the supervisor should add any difficult problems that are pending to a list of problems that "belong" to the whole workplace, not just to line or staff (see Figure 5-9). He or she should determine their priority on the basis of the amount of potential improvement and the effort it will take to bring it about. To develop and implement solutions, the supervisor should bring together project teams composed of both line workers and staff members. A cooperative approach during problem solving itself will lead to great progress in making effective workplace improvements. In most cases it is good to assign a line supervisor or a trained worker to act as project leader.

Figure 5-9.   Using the Big 3 Memo in an Improvement Project

Number	Number of problems not yet solved	Detected by:	Expected savings	Estimated cost	Implementation potential (level of difficulty)	Priority	Project leader	Worksite Members	Time period	Comments

Employee A — Big 3 Memo — Not yet solved — Solved immediately
Employee B — Big 3 Memo — Not yet solved — Solved immediately
Employee C — Big 3 Memo — Not yet solved — Solved immediately

Total number of problems detected and entered on a Big 3 Memo but not yet solved

Big 3 Improvement Plan Table

Joint strategy involving both line and staff members

Target: a standardized and highly efficient worksite

Line supervisors should recognize that even a little waste is too much. Using staff members effectively to help solve more difficult problems on the line is an important managerial skill to develop. An improvement strategy that line workers and staff members develop together will use everyone's abilities to better advantage — and take some of the emotion out of problem solving.

8. Keep Improvement Notes Together and Organized in the Big 3 Memo Workbook

We have been using the Big 3 Memo at Yamaha for more than ten years. When we first began using it, we just had single sheets of paper, not the workbook we use today. Frequently people would begin writing the memo form but quit in the middle. When I asked one worker why he didn't complete the form, he said, "I gave up because it's just the same old thing as making suggestions, and it's too much trouble to keep track of all the details on loose pieces of paper while I think about solutions."

It concerned me a lot that people were turned off by the memo. When I thought about how to present it better, I realized that

- Using this memo is different from simply writing improvement suggestions, and we needed a way to convey that.
- This memo is part of a system for observing and detecting problems.
- Memos written on single pieces of paper can get lost.

I started thinking about other operations where it is important that records are not misplaced. Imagine the messes and frustration that would result if banking transaction records were kept on loose paper slips. Banks provide passbooks to keep the records all in one place. Why not have a similar "passbook" form for employees to use when they "deposit" their ideas?

That was how the Big 3 Memo workbook was born. The workbook provides many blank forms, bound together, along with log sheets and a handbook section giving useful ideas about observing and solving problems. It is a tangible record that each employee can call his or her own and take pride in filling up with original observations and insights.

After people started recording their observations in the notebooks, it became easier to use the information and the number of memo-writers gradually increased. When I look at the files of all the memo volumes we have collected at Yamaha, I am impressed with the enthusiasm for improvement they represent. Even long-standing problem points were tackled. The memos express the individuality and different creative approaches of the people who made them. Naturally, I am very proud of the people who wrote them.

Foreman Tohru Kaneko of Yamaha Motor Manufacturing Factory Number 5 attaches a wide index tab to each memo page when he first makes a problem observation on the top of the memo form (see Figure 5-10). When he completes one side of the page with an implemented improvement, he clips the tab in half, leaving a narrower tab. When he implements an improvement for the memo on the other side, he clips off the other half. The number of tabs and half-tabs sticking out makes it obvious how many problems still need solving and makes it easier to look them up to think about them. Using this system personalizes a notebook, showing the writer's participation in the improvement process. The notebook becomes a tangible record of successes in making the workplace problem-free.

9. Use the Memo in Small Group Activities

Small group activities in the workplace are becoming more important in companies all over the world, not just in manufacturing industries but also in the service industry, white-collar work, and government agencies. Many of these groups have quality control and workplace improvement as their primary focus.

To promote these ends, a group typically starts out by drawing up a list of problem points for a particular workplace. From the list, the group chooses a theme to work on.

Too often, a group will rush out to make posters and displays about workplace problems before they understand what their problems really are. There is nothing wrong with a poster campaign, but first the group should study the actual problems to understand them as concretely as possible. When posters and

Figure 5-10. Foreman Kaneko's Memo System

BIG 3 MEMO

File No.

Plant:

Example of using index tabs

Name:	Section:	Worksite:	Group:
Tohru Kaneko		Production no. 1	

Machine Type:	Line/Parts:	Process:
J38		Crank assembly location guide

One side of the page has been completed, so half is cut off

Observation Points:

Point — equipment

-free Engineering — Strain-free

Big 3 Problem — Irrationality / Inconsistency / Waste

Present Condition

December 2, 1986

line

chute

guide

crank assembly

problem area

Neither side is done, so the whole tab is left

Observation:

When the crank assembly buckets move along the guide toward the chute, they sometimes get stuck. An operator has to reach in to unstick them, which creates a strain and is inefficient. This happens about 15 times a day.

After Improvements:

A piece is removed from the top guide, and the bottom guide is curved to move the bucket in the right direction. A hydraulic piston is installed to help the buckets move along smoothly.
34 area cut off

After Improvement

January 8, 1987

area cut off

piston

curve added

Improvements completed on both sides, so tab is completely cut off

Improvement Points

Eliminated problem of bucket getting stuck (the safety guide had become an unsafe guide).

Results

0.11 min. x $.19/min. x 15 times/day x 20 days = 6.27
Safety improvement

Cost Savings/Gain:

Improved safety + $6.27

Suggestion No.

Grade:

slogans are made up, they should address the actual problem points the employees have observed, such as "There are too many defective products," or "Operation X requires too much walking."

In my opinion, the most effective way to draw up a list of concrete problem points for the group to work with is to use the Big 3 Memo (see Figure 5-11). A number of companies are conducting small group activities using the Big 3 Memo. I would like to present two examples of their accomplishments.

Example 1

The people in this group work for a production control business division in a medium-sized enterprise. They began their improvement activities by choosing problem areas to focus on. Since they did not know how to proceed, they decided to use the Big 3 Memo as a guideline. In March 1987, group members attended a Zero Defects conference in Nagoya, Japan, and presented their results for discussion. Following is a summary of one of their presentations (see Figure 5-12):

- Company: Hamamatsu-shi Johoku Textile, Ltd.
- Worksite: Production Control Section
- Team: "Seikan-ers"
- Focus: Improving business procedures using the Big 3 Memo
- Time period: May 1984 to October 1986
- Main activities:
  - A Big 3 Memo notebook is kept in the work area for group members to use.
  - Whoever notices a problem writes it down on a memo page.
  - The group meets regularly to study the details of a problem, exchange ideas, and then consider countermeasures.
  - The group delegates implementation tasks among group members and then proceeds to make the improvement.
  - Many small problems can add up to a big savings. The chart in Figure 5-13 shows monthly cost savings resulting from improvements using this program.

Using the Big 3 Memo made it easy to continue these activities without making a big deal out of it. This group found it

Figure 5-11. Using the Big 3 Memo in Small Group Activities

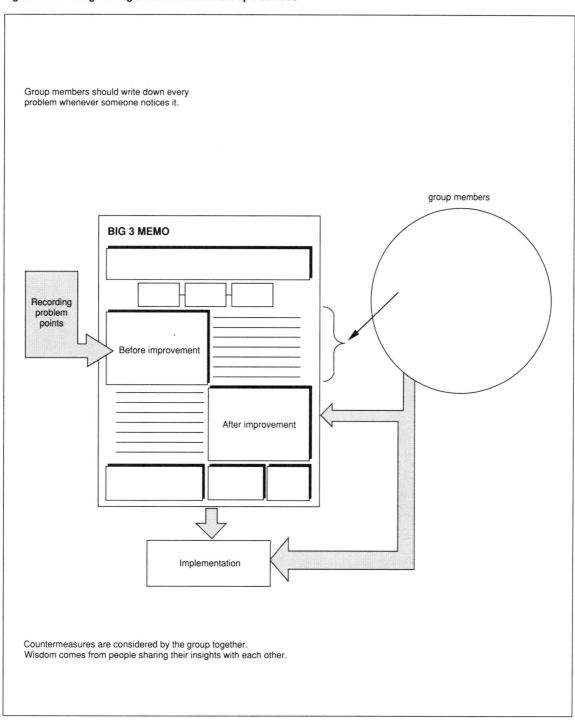

Figure 5-12. Big 3 Memo by a Production Control Group

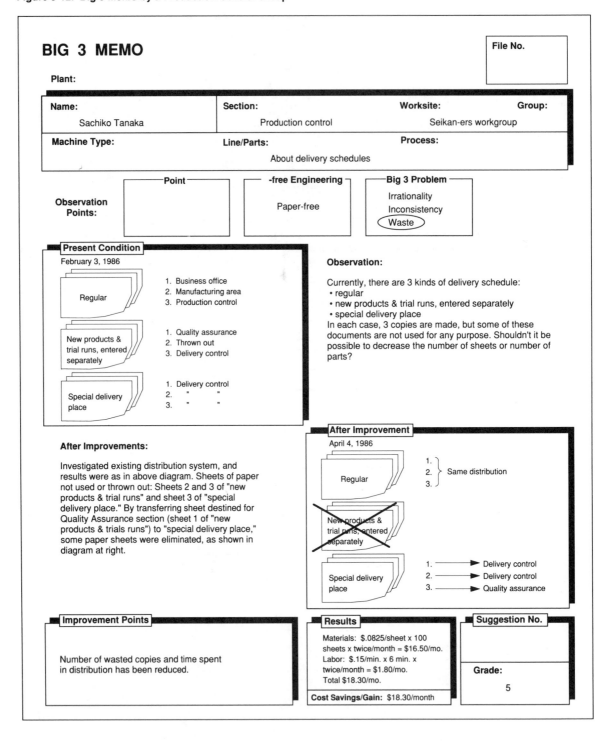

Figure 5-13. Savings from Small Group Problem-solving at Hamamatsu-shi Johoku Textile, Ltd.

	Problems detected	Solutions	Savings/month*
May-Oct. '84	7	4	¥12,995 ($57)
Nov. '84-Apr. '85	28	12	¥42,977 ($189)
May-Oct '85	30	11	¥421,891 ($1860)
Nov. '85-Apr. '86	48	21	¥9,948 ($44)
May-Oct. '86	17	9	¥22,350 ($98)

* Since the yen/dollar rates fluctuated substantially during the period of this chart, a fictitious single average value of ¥227.15/dollar has been used to underscore the comparison here (the arithmetic mean of the yen value on the first business day of each of the three years included). -- Ed.

helpful to learn more about quality control methods in order to develop good solutions. One way to use time designated for small group activities is to form study groups to learn to use the seven QC tools and the seven new QC tools.★ Figure 5-14 is a Pareto diagram of the types of problem-free engineering problems the group dealt with.

★ The seven QC tools are basic techniques for gathering and presenting data about problem points. These include Pareto diagrams, histograms, scatter diagrams, cause-and-effect (fishbone) diagrams, bar graphs, check sheets, and control charts (see Appendix Figure A-8). The first six of these tools are introduced in *The Idea Book* (Productivity Press, 1988), a handbook for total employee involvement using a participative suggestion system.

The seven new QC tools are a set of graphing and diagramming methods that aid in planning by organizing diverse data and clarifying complex causal relationships. These tools are described in *Managing for Quality Improvement: The 7 New QC Tools* (Productivity Press, 1988), Shigeru Mizuno, Ed. Both books are available from Productivity Press. — Ed.

Figure 5-14. Pareto Chart: Types of Problems Solved by the Production Control Group

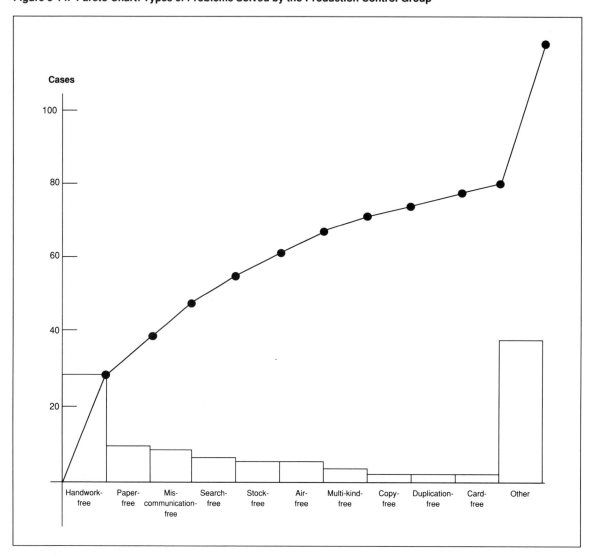

Example 2

At a May 1987 QC Circle Convention in Shizuoka Prefecture, Keiji Takada of the Nippondenso compressor manufacturing division, production section 2, "Siren" circle, delivered a paper titled "Activities to Improve Papering Operations Around the Inside of Housing Rotors." Following are some of his findings.

The housing rotor papering process had a very long tact time. Because this used a lot of labor time, the group set reduced time as its objective. Even though it was summer, a peak production time, the housing rotor papering group adopted the slogan, "Let's work hard together so we can all go home at the same time!"

The group started out using a histogram, or distribution diagram, one of the seven QC tools. It soon realized that this is a good method for showing results over time, but a more immediate way was needed to learn to detect the three basic problems quickly and come up with countermeasures that would help shorten the tact time.

This group decided to form study groups using the Big 3 Memo as a quick way to develop problem-finding skills. The notebook suggested to "observe carefully for five minutes." The group members came up with the idea of looking around the workplace through a megaphone to focus their concentration as much as possible while they kept in mind the basic problems they were trying to detect (see Figure 5-15A). This is a variation of the suggestion made in Chapter 4 to reduce distractions by observing through a tube.

Using this method, workers were able to detect problems they had not noticed before. The group then drew up an improvement plan, evaluating the effectiveness of various countermeasure proposals and the time they would take to implement. Individual responsibilities were assigned and the improvement proposals were then carried out.

Problem points detected using the megaphone strategy were improved during Strategies I and II, bringing the efficiency index down from 121 to 102. But the process still took longer than the objective of 100, so group members picked up the megaphones again and took another look. This led to Strategy

Figure 5-15. Group Improvement Activities at Nippondenso

A. Big 3 Memo Study Groups and the "Megaphone Strategy"

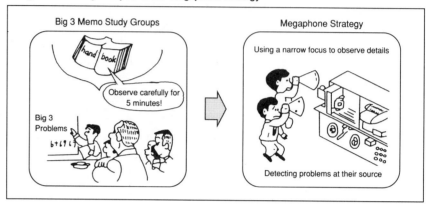

B. Achieving Efficiency

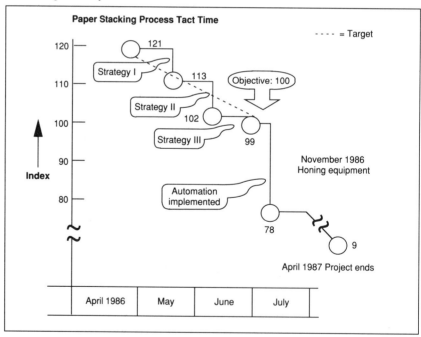

III (petitioning management for a paper-stacking machine), which brought the index to 99. Finally, management decided to further automate the related honing process. With automation, the index was finally reduced to 78. The focus on observing details had paid off: at last everyone could go home at the same time.

---

10. Use the Memo as a Source of Creative and Innovative Ideas

In Chapter 4, I described a television panel of senior production workers who were talking about how to make innovative ideas. As they saw it, these creative ideas begin with jotting down simple memos about problems such as daily tasks that are frustrating, inconvenient, or hard to do. Jobs that make workers feel uneasy and resigned to constant failure, work that takes backbreaking labor, and many other situations are the source of innovations in the workplace — but only if someone takes the time to report on them.

The Big 3 Memo is one of the best ways to do this. The problems should be written on memo forms as soon as they are noticed. Keeping these memos available in a notebook as a workbook for solution helps people keep the problems in mind for creating solutions and using new methods. This leads to many creative and inventive ideas.

CHAPTER 6

Examples of Problem-free Engineering

Examples 6–1 through 6–33

"If you are not making a conscious effort to observe things, you may be looking at them, but you really won't be seeing them." This old saying has some extraordinary implications. In other words, if you are not problem-conscious when you look at things, you just won't notice that something is wasteful, no matter how wasteful it actually is. When I look back at my own experiences, I know there were many times when I also overlooked waste.

However, after developing an awareness of the "big 3" problems (irrationality, inconsistency, and waste), I notice things and think about whether some problem is involved. With this framework, waste is not just an abstract idea. Rather it is something concrete, something that always needs to be probed a little more thoroughly, recognizing each case for what it is.

The rest of this chapter is devoted to illustrated examples of waste observed by using this " -free engineering" approach and of improvements that resulted. These examples are useful in helping operators and supervisors develop the problem-consciousness to detect waste.

Example 6-1: *Look*-free Engineering	**Subject: Personnel**

Points Involved:

- Automatic equipment has been installed, but the operator doesn't know how to use it

- Operation distribution is bad, so things are probably piling up

- An operator-machine chart has not been done

- The automatic stop device is not being used

Expected Benefits:

- Operators can program the same machines to perform many operations, cutting costs

- The job can be completed with fewer workers

- Increases productivity

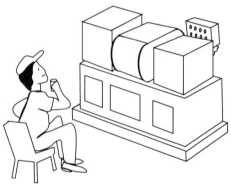

Latest model high-performance machinery going to waste.

No.	Process	Machine	Handling time	Machine time	Processing time	Cycle time: 0.2 0.4 0.6 0.8 1.0 1.2 1.4 1.6 1.8 2.0
1	Planing surface AB	Rotary	0.35	0.80	0.80	
2	Making reference holes	Special machine	0.10	0.65	0.75	walking
3	Tensioner	Special machine	0.10	0.66	0.76	
4	Press fitting holes B O.1	B.O	0.20	0.70	0.90	
5	Press fitting holes B O.2	B.O	0.25	0.65	0.95	
6	Pressure inspection	Leak tester	0.15	0.75	0.90	Operator A
7	Press fitting	Press fitter	0.20	0.70	0.90	
8	Planing surface A	Rotary	0.30	0.95	0.95	
9	Tapping surface A	Special machine	0.08	0.72	0.80	Operator B

Example 6-2: *Wasted motion*-free Engineering (1)	Subject: Personnel

Points Involved:

- Eliminating awkward operations
- Using operations with high motion economy
- Improving positions of materials, tools, workbenches, etc.

Expected Benefits:

- Decreases fatigue
- Eliminates motion-wasting operations
- Increases efficiency
- Improves quality
- Improved safety

Using both hands rhythmically

Left and right hands move unnaturally

Limiting the range of horizontal or vertical motion required

maximum

usual

Using both arms to balance the load

Using seated position to reduce fatigue

Using counter-height workbench

Using a holder to support weight

Rather than hammer hard with a small hammer, hammer lightly with a larger hammer

Using open parts box for easy grabbing

Easy to insert   Easy to insert   Hard to insert

Example 6-3: *Wasted motion* -free Engineering (2)

Subject: Personnel

Points Involved:

- Eliminating awkward operations
- Using operations with high motion economy
- Improving positions of materials, tools, workbenches, etc.

Expected Benefits:

- Decreases fatigue
- Eliminates motion-wasting operations
- Increases efficiency
- Improves quality
- Improves safety

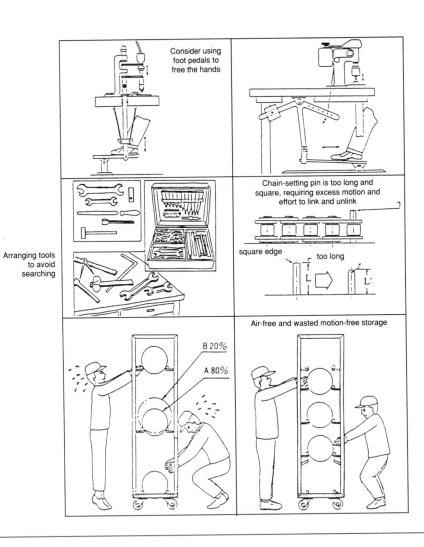

Consider using foot pedals to free the hands

Arranging tools to avoid searching

Chain-setting pin is too long and square, requiring excess motion and effort to link and unlink

square edge   too long

Air-free and wasted motion-free storage

B 20%

A 80%

Example 6-4: *Search*-free Engineering	Subject: Personnel (methods)

Points Involved:

- Does the need to look around for things result from inadequate cleaning and neatness?
- Can you place things so people won't have to search for them?
- Consider how to help everyone locate things quickly, using visual controls

Expected Benefits:

- The 5S principles are very helpful
- Eliminates waste caused by looking for things

The diagonal line makes sure a volume of work standards is returned to the right place -- no searching

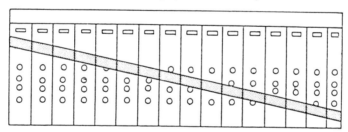

Use a wide range and shallow depth to cut down searching and lifting

Example 6-5: *Stack*-free Engineering	**Subject: Personnel (methods)**

Points Involved:

- Stacking blocks is a child's game
- Isn't it possible to operate without picking things up and stacking them?
- Is 1-unit flow possible?

Expected Benefits:

- Eliminates waste from taking and placing operations
- Reduces accumulation of materials
- Reduces physical strain and fatigue

Are you adding value or just stacking?

Spring-loaded hoppers eliminate wasteful walking and stacking

| Example 6-6: *Walk*-free Engineering (1) | Subject: Personnel (equipment) |

Points Involved:

- Lack of integration among moving, walking, and working operations
- 2 or 3 steps at a time can add up to a large total distance walked per day
- Can't the layout be changed to shorten the walking distance?

Expected Benefits:

- Reduces number of workers needed for one operation
- Uses multiple machines for efficient operation
- Uses space rationally

Is walking part of the job?

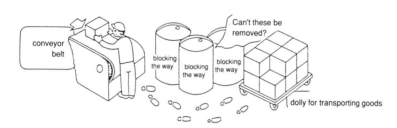

Let's devise a layout to cut down walking distance

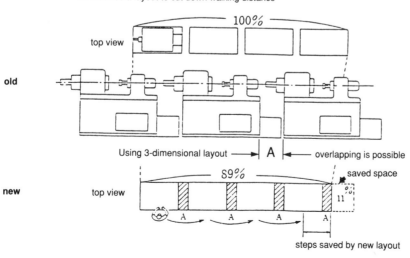

Example 6-7: *Walk*-free Engineering (2)

Subject: Personnel (equipment)

Points Involved:

• Can't the layout be changed to shorten the walking distance?

Expected Benefits:

• Eliminates wasted steps
• Shortens cycle time

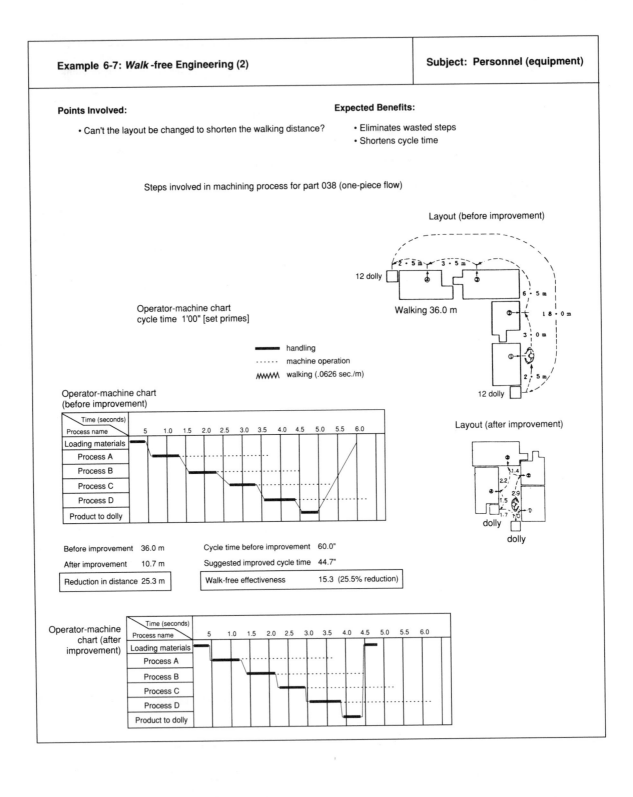

Steps involved in machining process for part 038 (one-piece flow)

Layout (before improvement)

12 dolly

Operator-machine chart
cycle time 1'00" [set primes]

Walking 36.0 m

⎯⎯ handling
...... machine operation
ᴡᴡᴡ walking (.0626 sec./m)

12 dolly

Operator-machine chart
(before improvement)

Time (seconds) Process name	5	1.0	1.5	2.0	2.5	3.0	3.5	4.0	4.5	5.0	5.5	6.0
Loading materials												
Process A												
Process B												
Process C												
Process D												
Product to dolly												

Layout (after improvement)

dolly

dolly

Before improvement	36.0 m
After improvement	10.7 m
Reduction in distance	25.3 m

Cycle time before improvement	60.0"
Suggested improved cycle time	44.7"
Walk-free effectiveness	15.3 (25.5% reduction)

Operator-machine
chart (after
improvement)

Time (seconds) Process name	5	1.0	1.5	2.0	2.5	3.0	3.5	4.0	4.5	5.0	5.5	6.0
Loading materials												
Process A												
Process B												
Process C												
Process D												
Product to dolly												

| Example 6-8: *Air* -free Engineering | Subject: Equipment |

Points Involved:

- Avoid transporting air
- Avoid making empty spaces
- Getting rid of empty space that generates no added value

Expected Benefits:

- Rationalizes flow
- Space can be used for a new operation, increasing the value of the workplace

How to avoid wasted space

For dollies to be transported by truck
If storage capacity doubles, transportation expenses will be cut in half

Restructure to use minimum required space

(example)

top view

50 units → 100 units

50 units → Saves roughly

space saved

$¥1,000-2,000/m^2$ ($7.50-15.00 @ ¥133/$)

Sliding shelf example

unnecessary space above

A

A'

Storage cartons

Don't be misled by external appearances

carton

Contains mostly air

Air

Use dividers to make multi-purpose box

when shelf spaces are not packed tightly

make another shelf

Example 6-9: *Conveyor*-free Engineering

Subject: Equipment

Points Involved:

- Has the conveyor become a flow operation with more showthan substance?
- Are there too many taking and placing operations?
- Is the surface of the conveyor being used only as a counter for parts?
- Do you really need a conveyor for 1-unit flow?

Expected Benefits:

- Frees unneeded space
- Decreases waste from taking and placing
- Decreases number of unfinished parts on the line

Using a counter for temporary holding

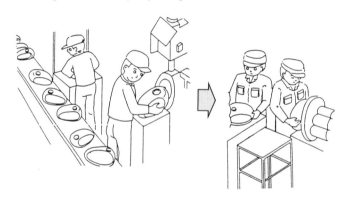

A conveyor requires taking and placing, even with an automatic feed machine

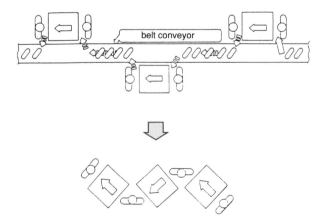

Example 6-10: *Air Press*-free Engineering	Subject: Equipment

Points Involved:

- Isn't there too much "air pressing" in press operations?
- Can't cylinder and ram movement be reduced?

Expected Benefits:

- Decreases cycle time
- Uses less energy
- Ultimately uses fewer pieces of equipment

Adjusting stopper and lowering dead center

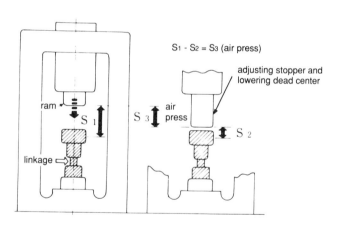

$S_1 - S_2 = S_3$ (air press)

Example of molding operation

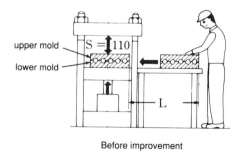

Before improvement

36% productivity increase from reduced pressing distance, reduced adjustment time, and more efficient loading

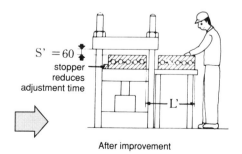

After improvement

Example 6-11: *Air Cut* -free Engineering	Subject: Equipment

Points Involved:

- Isn't some cutting wasted after the switch is turned on?
- Value is added only when the cutting sound can be heard
- Can waste of time outside of cutting time be eliminated?
- As far as possible, cut down time when operation is cutting nothing but air

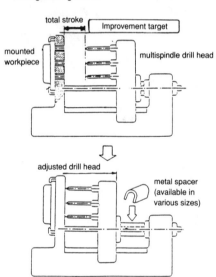

Expected Benefits:

- Decreases cycle time
- Uses less energy
- Ultimately uses fewer pieces of equipment

Automatic pipe cutter

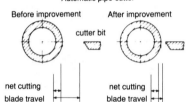

$T_1 - T_2 = T_3$
(minutes reduced)
$T_3 \div T_1 = X\%$ reduction

Before improvement

Task	Machine operation	Time
Cutting with bit	Blade unit forward	
	Cutting	
	Blade unit back	
	Remove work	
Cycle time	T'1	

$X\% =$ 20-50% efficiency improve ment

After improvement

Task	Machine operation	Time
Cutting with bit	Blade unit forward	
	Cutting	
	Blade unit back	
	Remove work	
Cycle time	T'2	

Improvement of NC turret drill

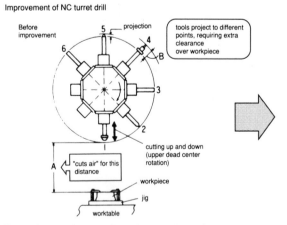

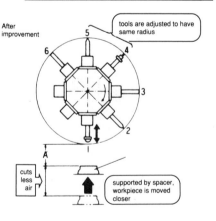

Example 6-12: *Air Grind* -free Engineering (1)	Subject: Equipment

Points Involved:

- Value is added only when the grinder is making sparks
- Do not be satisfied just because the machine is operating
- Cut down on time spent "grinding air"

Expected Benefits:

- Improves machine operation rate
- Increases productivity
- Reduces costs

Cutting grinder (grinder used for cutting)

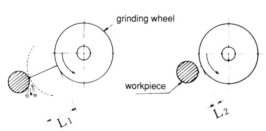

Note: Grinding wheels used for cutting become smaller due to abrasion and need periodic adjustments

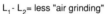

$L_1 - L_2 =$ less "air grinding"

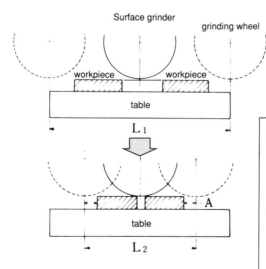

Operation standard (example)

1. When 2 articles are processed simultaneously, they are lined up with minimum space between them

2. Table movement is preset for shorter distance

Example 6-13: *Air Grind* -free Engineering (2)

Subject: Equipment

Points Involved:

- Value is added only when the grinder is making sparks
- Do not be satisfied just because the machine is operating
- Cut down on time spent "grinding air"

Expected Benefits:

- Improves machine operation rate
- Increases productivity
- Reduces costs

Improving a gear bore internal grinder

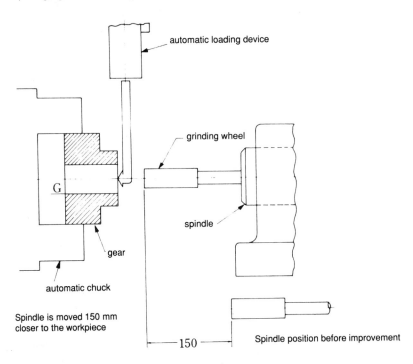

automatic loading device

grinding wheel

spindle

G

gear

automatic chuck

Spindle is moved 150 mm
closer to the workpiece

150

Spindle position before improvement

┌─ Effects ───┐

1,200 pieces manufactured per day ---- 1,400 pieces manufactured per day

UP approximately 17%

└──┘

Example courtesy of Toyo Seiki, Ltd.

Example 6-14: *Air Stroke* -free Engineering	Subject: Equipment

Points Involved:

- Is there waste from unnecessarily operating auxiliary equipment?
- Be more careful about operating things such as shutters, loaders, cylinders, etc.

Expected Benefits:

- Decreases cycle time
- Increases productivity
- Reduces costs

Small-scale coater improvement

Schematic drawing of coater

Time analysis for 1 cycle

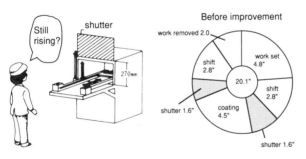

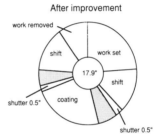

Before improvement

After improvement

Improved time by making shutter opening dimensions smaller

—Improvement contents—

Stopper installed keeps shutter from rising more than necessary

Results:

1% productivity increase from reducing wasted shutter stroke

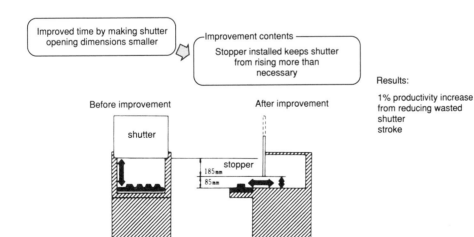

Before improvement

After improvement

Example courtesy of Imasen Electric, Hamakita Factory

Example 6-15: *Corner*-free Engineering	**Subject: Equipment**

Points Involved:

• Eliminating the problem of cleaning hard-to-reach places

Expected Benefits:

• Rationalizes cleaning operations to streamline workplace

Manufacturing often produces dirt and shavings that must be cleaned

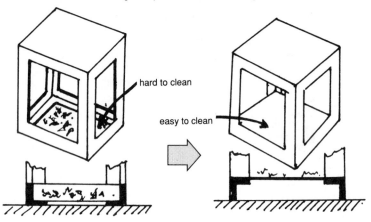

Wrap and suspend cords and pipes

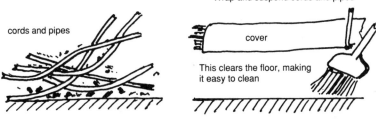

Closed pallet ends make cleanup easier

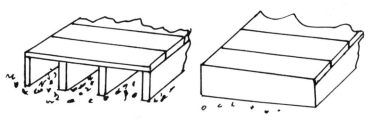

Example 6-16: *Oil Pan* -free Engineering

Subject: Equipment

Points Involved:

- Oil pans are not necessary unless there are oil leaks
- Learn to identify the causes of oil leaks

Expected Benefits:

- 5S can be more effective
- A completely efficient workplace can be achieved

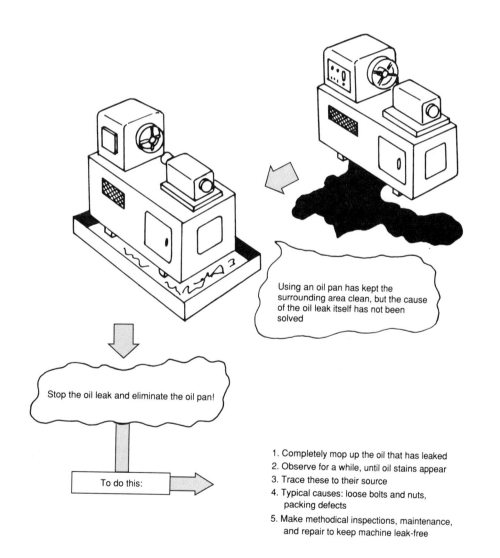

Using an oil pan has kept the surrounding area clean, but the cause of the oil leak itself has not been solved

Stop the oil leak and eliminate the oil pan!

To do this:

1. Completely mop up the oil that has leaked
2. Observe for a while, until oil stains appear
3. Trace these to their source
4. Typical causes: loose bolts and nuts, packing defects
5. Make methodical inspections, maintenance, and repair to keep machine leak-free

Example 6-17: *Short Stop* -free Engineering (1)	Subject: Equipment

Points Involved:

- Detecting short line stops and identifying causes
- Recognizing that short stops cause serious losses

Expected Benefits:

- Increases yield
- Decreases number of machines needed
- Increases productivity, decreases number of workers
- Avoids production of defective goods

Principles of short stop-free engineering

1. (Correcting very small defects that stop the machine)

Dust
×
Dirt
×
Levelness
×
Surface roughness

— Multiplied effect ➡ Losses up to 20 to 50%

Taking very small defects seriously:

Are there nearly invisible defects?

Recognize the importance of correcting borderline cases one by one and reducing short stops to zero.

2. (Determining the optimum standard)

External configuration

Materials

Dimensional accuracy

6 factors to study

Environmental conditions

Assembly accuracy

Use conditions

Studying how things should be:

Deciding the most suitable conditions and the limits of precision required for external shape and dimensions

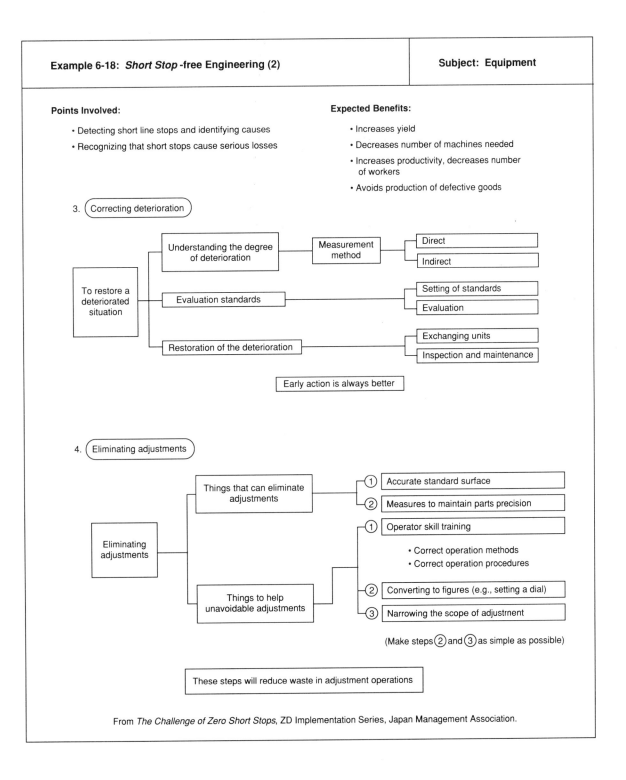

| Example 6-18: *Short Stop* -free Engineering (2) | Subject: Equipment |

Points Involved:

- Detecting short line stops and identifying causes
- Recognizing that short stops cause serious losses

Expected Benefits:

- Increases yield
- Decreases number of machines needed
- Increases productivity, decreases number of workers
- Avoids production of defective goods

3. Correcting deterioration

To restore a deteriorated situation
- Understanding the degree of deterioration — Measurement method — Direct / Indirect
- Evaluation standards — Setting of standards / Evaluation
- Restoration of the deterioration — Exchanging units / Inspection and maintenance

Early action is always better

4. Eliminating adjustments

Eliminating adjustments
- Things that can eliminate adjustments — ① Accurate standard surface — ② Measures to maintain parts precision
- Things to help unavoidable adjustments — ① Operator skill training
  - Correct operation methods
  - Correct operation procedures
  — ② Converting to figures (e.g., setting a dial)
  — ③ Narrowing the scope of adjustment

(Make steps ② and ③ as simple as possible)

These steps will reduce waste in adjustment operations

From *The Challenge of Zero Short Stops*, ZD Implementation Series, Japan Management Association.

Example 6-19: *Dust* -free Engineering	Subject: Equipment

Points Involved:

- Preventing scattering of dust, etc., at the source of the problem

Expected Benefits:

- Improves environment
- Improves quality
- Increases productivity

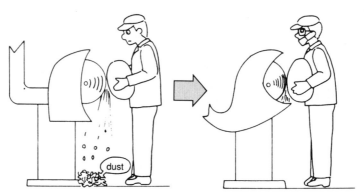

Is the cover functioning as a dust remover?

Reconstructed so that dust is sucked in

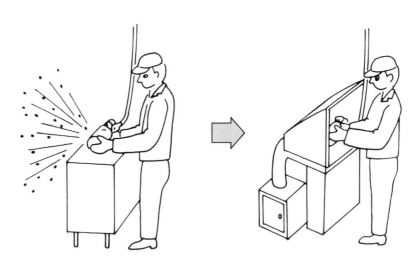

| **Example 6-20:** *Toolbox*-free Engineering | **Subject: Tools** |

Points Involved:

- Is it necessary to use toolboxes that hide what they contain?
- Method of arranging tools so users can easily understand where they are

Expected Benefits:

- Eliminates having too many or too few tools
- Eliminates waste of looking for things

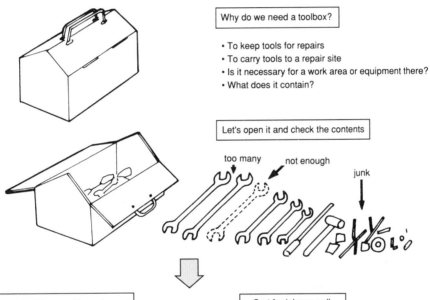

Why do we need a toolbox?

- To keep tools for repairs
- To carry tools to a repair site
- Is it necessary for a work area or equipment there?
- What does it contain?

Let's open it and check the contents

too many   not enough   junk

Things required for specific equipment

Cart for jobs on call

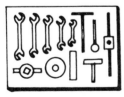

- Minimum tools required
- Easy to understand
- Arranged so missing items will be noticed immediately

Quick Changeover Cart

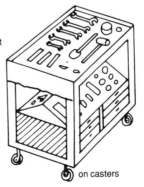

- Required tools, measuring devices, materials, guides, etc.

on casters

Example 6-21: *Bottleneck* -free Engineering	Subject: Methods

Points Involved:

- Identifying bottleneck processes where materials are piling up and causing delays before the process itself
- Among consecutive operations, which ones require the most time?
- Are bottlenecks affecting quality, cost, or delivery?
- Devising ways of immediately eliminating bottlenecks

Expected Benefits:

- Rearranging the order of bottleneck processes promotes smoother flow
- Enables planning for reduced cycle time
- Reduces the number of unfinished parts on the line

Process	D M	Time (in .01 min.) 10 20 30 40 50
1	40	
2	35	
3	40	
4	50	
5	42	
6	38	
7	43	

- Analyze bottleneck processes
- Is the operation distribution appropriate?
- Can people in prior and/or subsequent processes give some help?
- Maintain the overall balance

Is something stopping the flow?

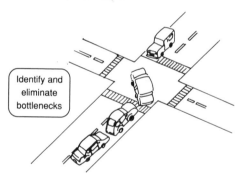

Identify and eliminate bottlenecks

Can people work together to make things flow smoothly?

| Example 6-22: *Inventory* -free Engineering | Subject: Methods |

Points Involved:

- Using a flow curve graph, get a clear understanding of the lead time and the amount of inventory

- After grasping the relationship between estimates and actual results, work out a system to prevent excess production

- Construct a system capable of making whatever customer want whenever they want it

- Inventory is a mountain of money

- Can a kanban system be used?

Expected Benefits:

- Possible to carry less inventory

- Uses the law of supply and demand to prevent overstocking

- Promotes fundamentally stronger management

- Improves reserve funds

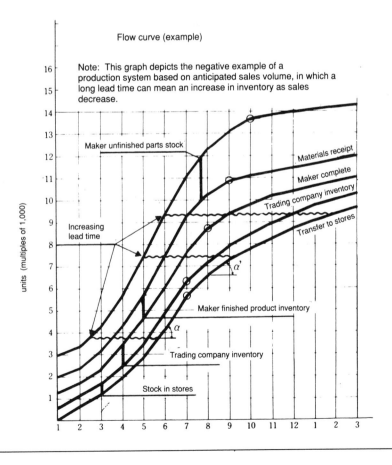

Flow curve (example)

Note: This graph depicts the negative example of a production system based on anticipated sales volume, in which a long lead time can mean an increase in inventory as sales decrease.

Example 6-23: *Hunger*-free Engineering	Subject: **Methods**

Points Involved:

- Is the machine "hungry," just waiting to receive materials?
- Perform manual operations after providing the machine with materials
- Isn't it wasteful to combine the time for machine operations and manual operations?

Expected Benefits:

- Improves machine operation rate
- Reduces cycle time

Operator-machine chart

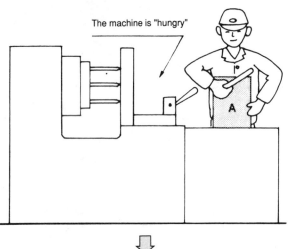

The machine is "hungry"

Time	Machine	Worker
		Turn off
		Remove A
	Machine is hungry	Manual operation on A
		Mount B,
		turn on
	B machining	Observation and waiting
		Turn off

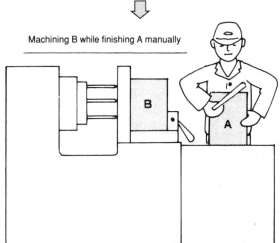

Machining B while finishing A manually

		Turn off
		Remove A
		Mount B
		Turn on
	B machining	Manual operation on A
		Turn off
		Remove B
		Mount C
		Turn on
	C machining	Manual operation on B

Example 6-24: *Changeover* -free Engineering	Subject: Methods

Points Involved:

- Production lots will become smaller, with more kinds of products turned out in smaller volumes
- Changeover must be improved to make small lot production profitable
- Making a profit-loss break-even graph

Expected Benefits:

- Gives a foothold for making changeover improvements
- Promotes clear understanding of the relationship between changeovers and profit-loss break-even points

Points to watch in making profit-loss break-even graphs

- The 45-degree line denotes standard time
- Make estimated parts processing time scale corresponding to number of units
- Treat changeover time as fixed cost
- Treat actual processing time as variable cost

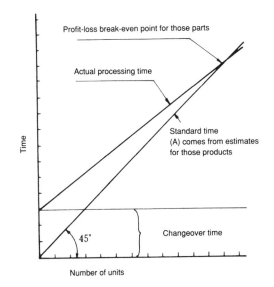

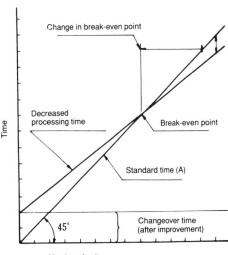

To improve changeover:

- Actual situation is investigated during an "open" changeover
- Develop countermeasures based on time analysis data
- Convert internal setup into external setup
- Begin with proper arrangement and good order in the die-changing area
- Clarify each person's role and responsibility

Useful aspects of problem-free engineering:

- Walk-free
- Search-free
- Wasted motion-free
- Bolt-free

Example 6-25: *Bolt*-free Engineering	Subject: Methods

Points Involved:

- Relation between number of assembly workers and number of bolts

- Using minimum required number of bolts

- Decreasing number of parts also decreases number of bolts

- Bolts add time to changeover operations

Expected Benefits:

- Major cost reductions

- Requires fewer changeover workers

- Decreases number of parts

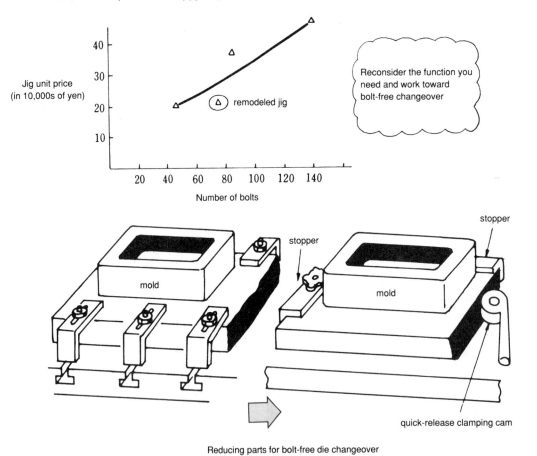

Relation between price of assembly jig unit price and number of bolts in jig

Jig unit price (in 10,000s of yen)

△ remodeled jig

Number of bolts

Reconsider the function you need and work toward bolt-free changeover

stopper

stopper

mold

mold

quick-release clamping cam

Reducing parts for bolt-free die changeover

Example 6-26: *Weight*-free Engineering	Subject: **Methods**

Points Involved:

- Can some weight be reduced and things made lighter?
- Would lighter materials be adequate for the job?
- Can heavy things be made easier to move?

Expected Benefits:

- Helps reduce costs
- Increases productivity
- Reduces fatigue and injury

(A)   (B)

B is lighter than A; to understand why,
examine the cross-section

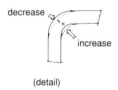

decrease

increase

(detail)

Weight-free design:

- Reduce the angle as much as possible
- Make cast items as thin as possible while maintaining necessary strength
- More and smaller ribs make it possible to decrease weight without sacrificing strength

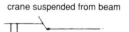

crane suspended from beam

air cylinder

Example of handling heavy objects more easily

500 units moved/day x 17 kg/unit = 8.5 t moved/day

grip

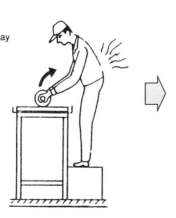

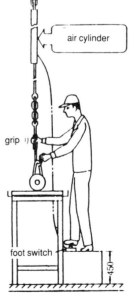

foot switch

450

Example courtesy of Yamaha Motor, Ltd., Iwata factory.

Example 6-27: *Burr*-free Engineering	Subject: Value Analysis

Points Involved:

- Deburring is a manual operation
- Designing dies and parts so that burrs do not occur
- Isn't it possible to do any necessary deburring as part of a subsequent process?

Expected Benefits:

- Increases productivity
- Improves quality
- Decreases work-in-process

Burr elimination example

upper die

Operation 1　　　product

lower die

(A-A' cross-section)

Operation 2　　　punch

product (top view)

makes burrs

Deburring requires 0.6 min./unit

Burr-free breakthrough!

Before improvement

Operation 1 lower die remodeled

After improvement

0.7 mm

makes
shallow dent,
leaving burr

1.7 mm

makes
deeper dent,
eliminating burr

Example courtesy of Yamaha Motor, Ltd., Hamakita factory, from the Big 3 Memo workbook of Kenji Ito.

Example 6-28: *Welding* -free Engineering	Subject: Value Analysis

Points Involved:

• Many welds means many workers
• Many welds result from having many part

Expected Benefits:

• Reduces costs
• Improves quality
• Increases productivity

Example of welding-free and parts-free (eliminating random parts)

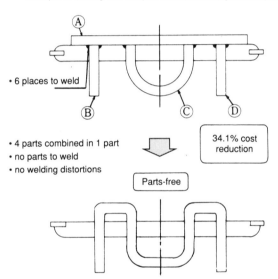

• 6 places to weld

• 4 parts combined in 1 part
• no parts to weld
• no welding distortions

34.1% cost reduction

Parts-free

Parts-free Engineering	Subject: Value Analysis

Points Involved:

• Can the number of parts be reduced?
• Can a single part be given multiple functions?

Expected Benefits:

• Reduces costs

Example 6-29: *Multiple Problem* -free Engineering | **Subject: Application**

Points Involved:

- Eliminating irrationality, waste, and inconsistency by combining functions
- Achieving multiple objectives kills several birds with one stone
- Consider several problems together for a strong result

Expected Benefits:

- The most effective solutions simultaneously resolve several problems at once
- This approach can produce practical and popular devices to make work easier

Example: a tool belt for electrical line work

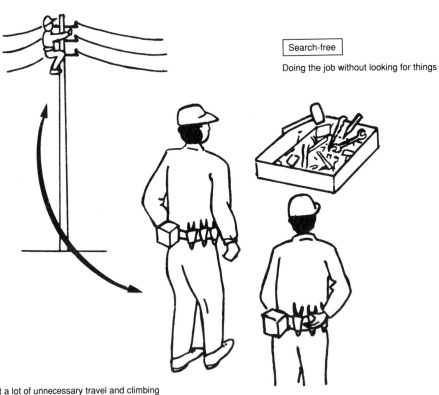

Search-free

Doing the job without looking for things

Walk-free

Doing the job without a lot of unnecessary travel and climbing

Wasted motion-free

Easy to get at tools right away

Example 6-30: *Accident* -free Engineering					Subject: Safety

Accident -free Engineering \ 4 Basic Elements	Personnel	Equipment	Materials	Method	
Roller accident-free					• Are shafts, joints, gears, chains, pulleys, belt drives, or high-speed rotating bodies in exposed areas? • Use safety countermeasures to prevent contact between rotating bodies and hands, fingers, uniforms, gloves, caps, or hair
Pinch-free					• Is there a risk of cuts, scrapes, or abrasions from such things as woodworking machines, milling machines, and grinders?
Cut-free					• Can things such as jigs, dies, work and machines get squeezed in between interlocking objects and fixed objects?
Crash-free					• Are there places where collisions could occur with forklifts, power transport machines, and other vehicles? • Are there passageways or corridors with broken floors or poor lighting? • Are there places where people could slip because of oil on floors? • Drivers and loaders must be careful to use slings properly for lifting work
Mis-step-free					• Are there places where people could slip on wood shavings, broken glass, nails, or bolts while passing by, or while they are performing operations involving on a platform?
Drop-free					• Is there a risk of dropping things on foot platforms, from ladders, on stairways, bridge passageways, or into pits or manholes?
Startle-free					• Is there a risk of places badly stacked or lined up things falling? • Is there a risk of dropping tools or supplies being used in high places?
Handling-accident-free					• Is there a risk of things falling down on top of people during loading, unloading, and transport? • When several workers manually transport heavy loads, caution must be exercised to prevent things from being dropped through strain, muscle stiffness, or stumbling; preparation and training are needed
PM accident-free					• Are some places dangerous due to irregular operations such as repair work? • Handling machines that are down, mounting and removing parts, and doing adjustment changeovers or product assembly analysis are mostly manual operations
Electric shock-free					• Are there places where grounding is inadequate, cords are exposed, and people touch wires without checking whether they are live or dead? • When electrical work involves shutting off electricity, a communication protocol must be followed to avoid shocks when power is restored
Poison-free					• Are there places where poisonous substances, acid vapors, dangerous gases, etc. are emitted environment? • Check in advance for poisonous gases or chemicals whenever performing operations in small enclosed rooms, pits, or tanks
Bomb-free					• Is there a risk of explosion from such things as dangerous substances, vapors, pressurized air, steam, high pressure gases, dust, static electricity, etc.? • Use countermeasures to prevent molten metal from falling into water accumulated on floors or in pits
Scar-free					• Is there a risk of contact with materials at very high or low temperatures (casting, forging, electric welding)? • Always use fire resistant gloves • Never perform such operations shirtless or without adequate foot protection • Shield face and eyes from light and heat injury from very hot furnaces; metals may still be very hot even when no longer red-hot
Overheating-free					• Are operations performed for long periods in high-temperature areas? • Use countermeasures to prevent illnesses resulting from heat
Fall-free					• Is there a risk of falling from structures, stacked materials, unsafe machine gantries and ladders, cranes, etc.?
Nonlicense-free					• Are operations being performed by people who lack licenses or other necessary qualifications required by the company?
Ignorance-free					• Are operations unsafe due to inadequate training or supervision?

Unmarked hazard-free					• Are signs or indicators marking those areas that can be most dangerous? Signs remind us of what to look for during times when we are noticing things. Use simple letters in several colors to attract attention.
					• Indicators for dangerous substances should include
					  1. Name of substance
					  2. Toxic or hazard level
					  3. Treatment outline
					  4. Indications for emergency treatment

Frustration-free					• Use countermeasures against mental and emotional symptoms that may arise due to job stresses and changing work situations • Organize a counseling program
_____-free					• Won't you also think of something to be included here?

Example 6-31: *Office Management Problem* -free Engineering (1)	Subject: Office

_____-free Engineering	Points Involved:	Expected Benefits:
Paper-free	Smooth arrangement and ordering of documents and bookshelves "Arrangement" means sorting out unneeded documents "Order" means organizing for immediate access to what is needed Document files centralized for common use Private supplies of office materials eliminated Can you use the reverse side of the paper too? Do you need all that computer output? Can you cut down your use of paper stock? Do you need paper of that size? Take advantage of office automation and computers	Can plan for rationalizing office management and office business Creates extra office space
Delivery cost-free	Is this letter necessary? Is special delivery necessary? Have you compared delivery services? Check carefully for correct contents and address	Reduce mailing expenses
Stamp-free	Do you have to stamp that document ? Can you reduce the instances when stamping is necessary?	Rationalizing office work
Make-work-free	Can the stamped information be preprinted on the form? Are you creating unnecessary work for yourself or others?	Rationalizing office employee systems
Wasted motion-free	Who is that activity helping? Isn't there some waste, irrationality, or inconsistency in operations from inefficient movements?	Rationalizing office operations
Walk-free	Why are so many people walking around in that office? Can mail deliveries be regularized? Can't you finish what you sat down to do? Can the layout be adjusted for less walking to stairs or entrances?	Office rationalization

Example 6-32: *Office Management Problem* -free Engineering		Subject: Office
_____-free Engineering	Points Involved:	Expected Benefits:
Call-free	Is a phone call necessary? Is there a clear distinction between company and private calls? Talk as little as possible; put things in writing Pay for your own telephone calls Avoid needless conversation and long calls	Lower telephone and telegram costs Creates extra office space
Bottleneck-free	Does something hold up the smooth flow of office business? If it takes many people to do the same job, that job becomes a bottleneck	Office rationalization
Meeting-free	Is that meeting necessary for the job? Avoid gossipy meetings and just shooting the breeze	Office rationalization
Overservice-free	Is that service responding to customer needs? Are the expenditures higher than necessary? Are you expressing a self-serving attitude? Spread good will with true service	Reduce entertainment expenses
Copy-free	Is that copy necessary? Can you use the back of the paper also?	Office rationalization
Irregularity-free	Are rules and regulations being observed? Why should you take special privileges? Are people getting worthwhile work done during specified times?	Reinforcing professional standards of behavior in the office
Look-free	Office automation improves nothing if people just sit watching the equipment as it is working Are you just staring? Are you thinking?	Office rationalization
Cash-free	Think of ways to avoid needing petty cash for the job	Office rationalization Avoiding errors in cash-handling and bookkeeping
Smoke-free	When people smoke, they stop working with their hands Ban smoking, or permit it only at certain times and places	Smoking is unhealthy for smokers and people around smokers

Example 6-33: *Energy*-free Engineering

Subject: General

Points Involved:

- Energy is limited
- Devise ways to reduce energy consumption, no matter how small

Expected Benefits:

- Efficient use of energy
- Lower costs

Energy-saving products for daily living

Solar water heater

Refrigerators: Separate compartment doors conserve energy

Cutting costs

Almost all of these "-free"s save energy and lower costs

CHAPTER 7

Examples of
the Big 3 Memo

Examples 7-1 through 7-30

During the past several years, I have collected a large number of Big 3 Memo examples during seminar training sponsored by the Japan Management Association. Some of these I would like to share with you here, with the permission of the writers. The original memos were written by hand, which is the most practical way to record these observations. In order to make the memos easier to read, however, we have typeset the handwriting.

Please examine these examples carefully. Even people familiar with the concepts underlying the Big 3 Memo are often surprised to find the actual memo-writing process so effective.

Example 7-1

BIG 3 MEMO

File No.

Plant: Komatsu Screw Manufacturing, Ltd.

Name: K. Suzuki	**Section:** Lumber	**Worksite:** Woodworking outer packaging	**Group:** 4
Machine Type: Piano	**Line/Parts:** Outer packaging	**Process:** Gluing	

Observation Points:

Point	**-free Engineering**	**Big 3 Problem**
Morning changeover	Look-free	Irrationality Inconsistency (Waste)

Present Condition

10/25/84

P1
P2   switch
P3   OFF
P4   waiting

25 min/day warm-up, inspection, etc. needed for each machine. Start: 8:05 (work starts: 8:30).

Observation:

Every morning it takes about 25 minutes to warm up the 4 gluing presses, make the glue, and do inspections. This prep work doesn't take all 12 workers, so some of this time is just idle waiting.

Per month: 25 min/day x 21 days = 525 min/month
525 min/month x 12 workers = 6,300 min/month labor (waste)

After Improvements:

3 workers arrive 30 minutes early to begin prep work, so that press can begin operating as soon as work begins.

30 min x 21 days = 630 min/month x 3 workers = 1,890 min labor

After Improvement

11/5/84

Start at 8:05

P1
P2
P3
P4

Start work at 7:30   Switch ON

Improvement Points

Machines and workers function more efficiently at starting time.

Results

6300 min. - 1890 min. = 4410 min. labor saved

Cost Savings/Gain:

$670/month

Suggestion No.

Grade:

Example 7-2

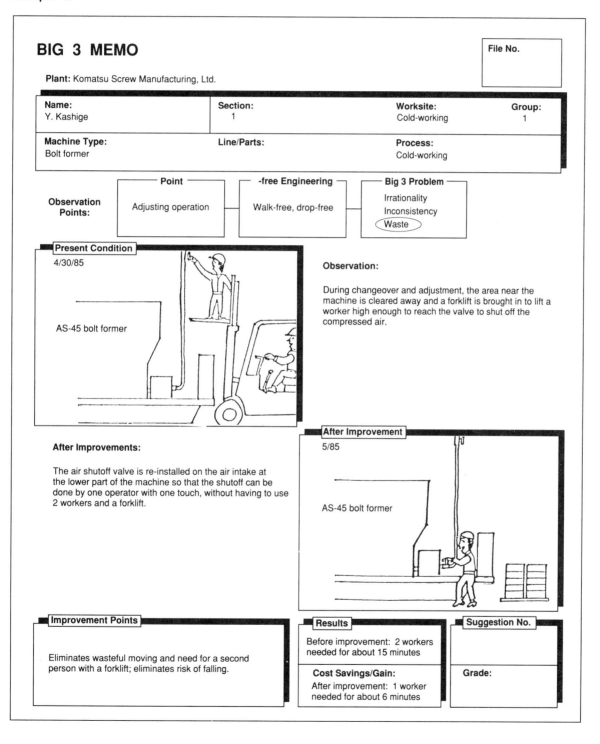

BIG 3 MEMO

File No.

Plant: Komatsu Screw Manufacturing, Ltd.

Name: Y. Kashige	Section: 1	Worksite: Cold-working	Group: 1
Machine Type: Bolt former	Line/Parts:	Process: Cold-working	

Observation Points:

- **Point** — Adjusting operation
- **-free Engineering** — Walk-free, drop-free
- **Big 3 Problem** — Irrationality / Inconsistency / (Waste)

Present Condition
4/30/85

AS-45 bolt former

Observation:

During changeover and adjustment, the area near the machine is cleared away and a forklift is brought in to lift a worker high enough to reach the valve to shut off the compressed air.

After Improvements:

The air shutoff valve is re-installed on the air intake at the lower part of the machine so that the shutoff can be done by one operator with one touch, without having to use 2 workers and a forklift.

After Improvement
5/85

AS-45 bolt former

Improvement Points

Eliminates wasteful moving and need for a second person with a forklift; eliminates risk of falling.

Results

Before improvement: 2 workers needed for about 15 minutes

Cost Savings/Gain:

After improvement: 1 worker needed for about 6 minutes

Suggestion No.

Grade:

Example 7-3

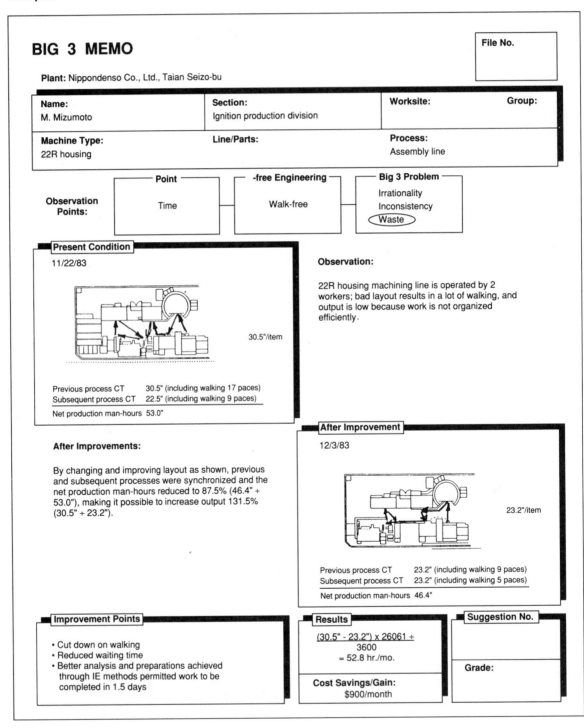

BIG 3 MEMO

File No.

Plant: Nippondenso Co., Ltd., Taian Seizo-bu

Name: M. Mizumoto	**Section:** Ignition production division	**Worksite:**	**Group:**
Machine Type: 22R housing	**Line/Parts:**	**Process:** Assembly line	

Observation Points:

Point	-free Engineering	Big 3 Problem
Time	Walk-free	Irrationality Inconsistency (Waste)

Present Condition

11/22/83

30.5"/item

Previous process CT	30.5" (including walking 17 paces)
Subsequent process CT	22.5" (including walking 9 paces)
Net production man-hours 53.0"	

Observation:

22R housing machining line is operated by 2 workers; bad layout results in a lot of walking, and output is low because work is not organized efficiently.

After Improvements:

By changing and improving layout as shown, previous and subsequent processes were synchronized and the net production man-hours reduced to 87.5% (46.4" ÷ 53.0"), making it possible to increase output 131.5% (30.5" ÷ 23.2").

After Improvement

12/3/83

23.2"/item

Previous process CT	23.2" (including walking 9 paces)
Subsequent process CT	23.2" (including walking 5 paces)
Net production man-hours 46.4"	

Improvement Points

- Cut down on walking
- Reduced waiting time
- Better analysis and preparations achieved through IE methods permitted work to be completed in 1.5 days

Results

$$\frac{(30.5" - 23.2") \times 26061}{3600} = 52.8 \text{ hr./mo.}$$

Cost Savings/Gain: $900/month

Suggestion No.

Grade:

Example 7-4

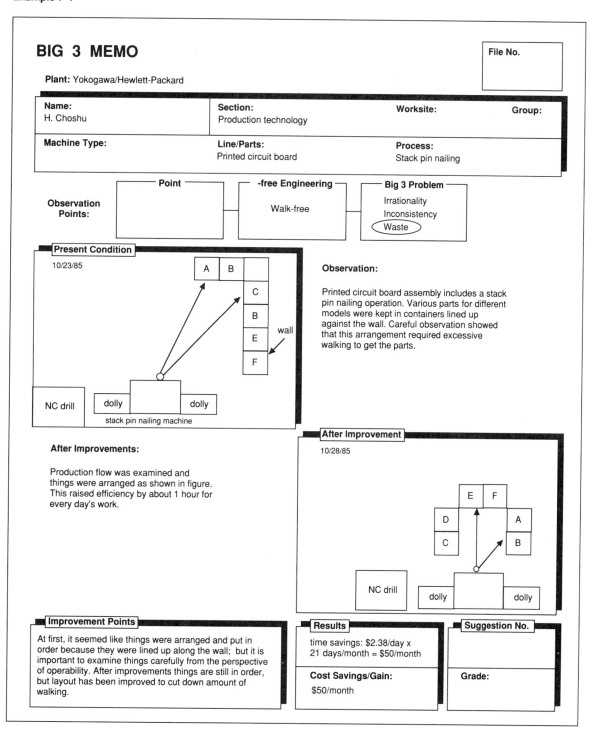

BIG 3 MEMO

File No.

Plant: Yokogawa/Hewlett-Packard

| **Name:** H. Choshu | **Section:** Production technology | **Worksite:** | **Group:** |
| **Machine Type:** | **Line/Parts:** Printed circuit board | **Process:** Stack pin nailing | |

Observation Points:

Point — -free Engineering — Big 3 Problem

Walk-free

Irrationality
Inconsistency
Waste

Present Condition

10/23/85

A B
C
B
E — wall
F

NC drill   dolly   dolly
stack pin nailing machine

Observation:

Printed circuit board assembly includes a stack pin nailing operation. Various parts for different models were kept in containers lined up against the wall. Careful observation showed that this arrangement required excessive walking to get the parts.

After Improvements:

Production flow was examined and things were arranged as shown in figure. This raised efficiency by about 1 hour for every day's work.

After Improvement

10/28/85

E F
D   A
C   B

NC drill   dolly   dolly

Improvement Points

At first, it seemed like things were arranged and put in order because they were lined up along the wall; but it is important to examine things carefully from the perspective of operability. After improvements things are still in order, but layout has been improved to cut down amount of walking.

Results

time savings: $2.38/day x
21 days/month = $50/month

Cost Savings/Gain:
$50/month

Suggestion No.

Grade:

Example 7-5

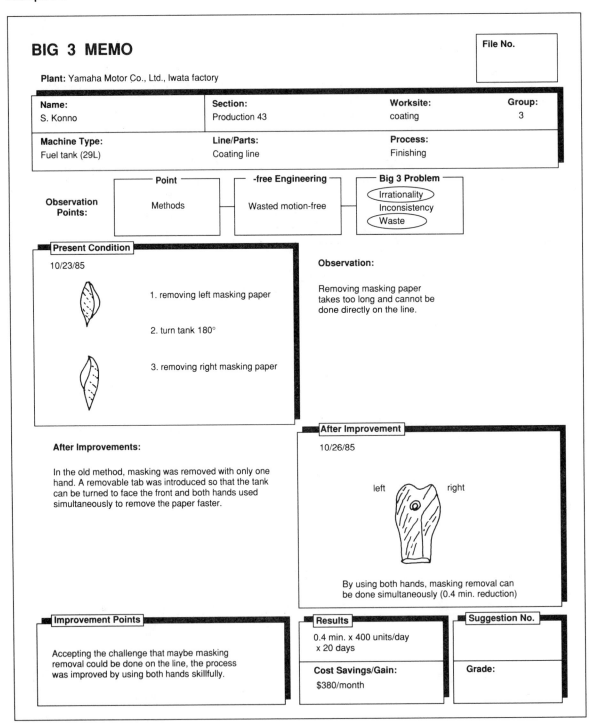

BIG 3 MEMO

File No.

Plant: Yamaha Motor Co., Ltd., Iwata factory

Name: S. Konno	**Section:** Production 43	**Worksite:** coating	**Group:** 3
Machine Type: Fuel tank (29L)	**Line/Parts:** Coating line	**Process:** Finishing	

Observation Points:

┌─ **Point** ─┐   ┌─ **-free Engineering** ─┐   ┌─ **Big 3 Problem** ─┐
│ Methods │   │ Wasted motion-free │   Irrationality
                                            Inconsistency
                                            Waste

Present Condition

10/23/85

1. removing left masking paper

2. turn tank 180°

3. removing right masking paper

Observation:

Removing masking paper takes too long and cannot be done directly on the line.

After Improvements:

In the old method, masking was removed with only one hand. A removable tab was introduced so that the tank can be turned to face the front and both hands used simultaneously to remove the paper faster.

After Improvement

10/26/85

left   right

By using both hands, masking removal can be done simultaneously (0.4 min. reduction)

Improvement Points

Accepting the challenge that maybe masking removal could be done on the line, the process was improved by using both hands skillfully.

Results

0.4 min. x 400 units/day x 20 days

Cost Savings/Gain:

$380/month

Suggestion No.

Grade:

Example 7-6

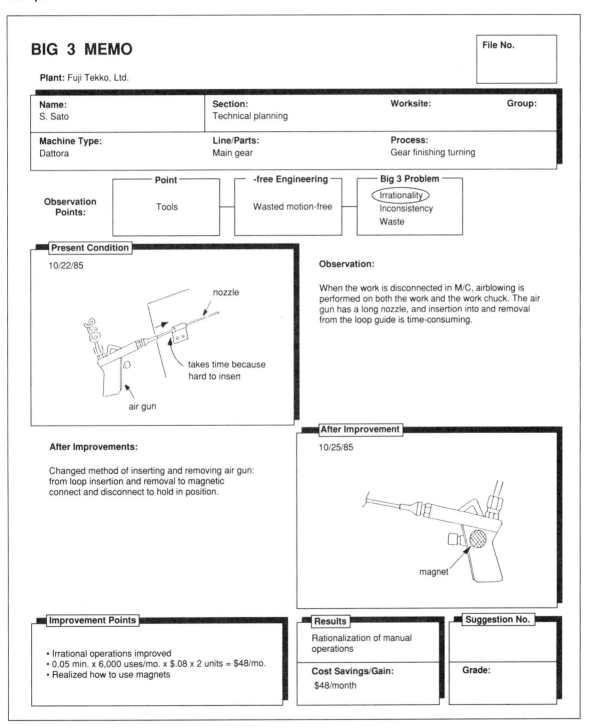

BIG 3 MEMO

File No.

Plant: Fuji Tekko, Ltd.

Name: S. Sato	**Section:** Technical planning	**Worksite:**	**Group:**
Machine Type: Dattora	**Line/Parts:** Main gear	**Process:** Gear finishing turning	

Observation Points:

┌─ **Point** ─┐   ┌─ **-free Engineering** ─┐   ┌─ **Big 3 Problem** ─┐
Tools   Wasted motion-free   (Irrationality)
                                                    Inconsistency
                                                    Waste

Present Condition

10/22/85

nozzle

takes time because hard to insert

air gun

Observation:

When the work is disconnected in M/C, airblowing is performed on both the work and the work chuck. The air gun has a long nozzle, and insertion into and removal from the loop guide is time-consuming.

After Improvements:

Changed method of inserting and removing air gun: from loop insertion and removal to magnetic connect and disconnect to hold in position.

After Improvement

10/25/85

magnet

Improvement Points

• Irrational operations improved
• 0.05 min. x 6,000 uses/mo. x $.08 x 2 units = $48/mo.
• Realized how to use magnets

Results

Rationalization of manual operations

Cost Savings/Gain:

$48/month

Suggestion No.

Grade:

Example 7-7

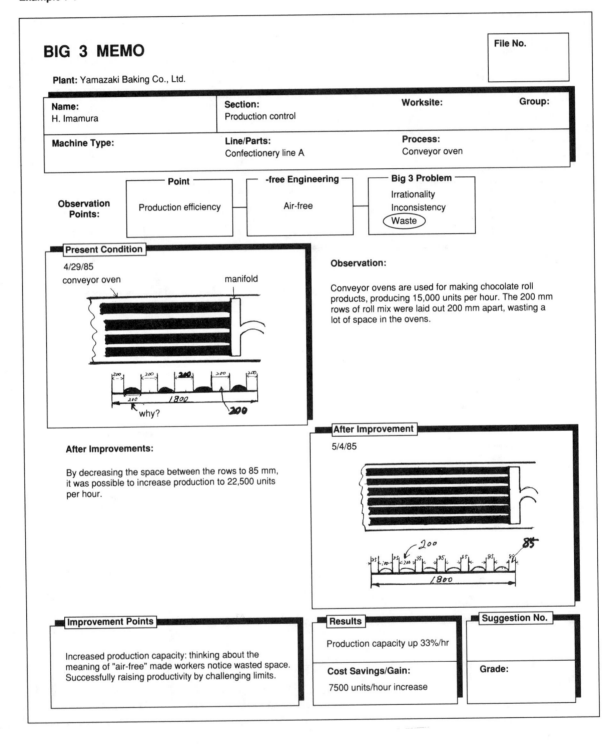

BIG 3 MEMO

File No.

Plant: Yamazaki Baking Co., Ltd.

| **Name:** H. Imamura | **Section:** Production control | **Worksite:** | **Group:** |

| **Machine Type:** | **Line/Parts:** Confectionery line A | **Process:** Conveyor oven |

Observation Points:

| **Point** Production efficiency | **-free Engineering** Air-free | **Big 3 Problem** Irrationality Inconsistency (Waste) |

Present Condition

4/29/85
conveyor oven   manifold

200   200   200   200   200
210   1800
why?   *200*

Observation:

Conveyor ovens are used for making chocolate roll products, producing 15,000 units per hour. The 200 mm rows of roll mix were laid out 200 mm apart, wasting a lot of space in the ovens.

After Improvements:

By decreasing the space between the rows to 85 mm, it was possible to increase production to 22,500 units per hour.

After Improvement

5/4/85

200
85
85   200   85   85   85   85   85
1800

Improvement Points

Increased production capacity: thinking about the meaning of "air-free" made workers notice wasted space. Successfully raising productivity by challenging limits.

Results

Production capacity up 33%/hr

Cost Savings/Gain:

7500 units/hour increase

Suggestion No.

Grade:

Example 7-8

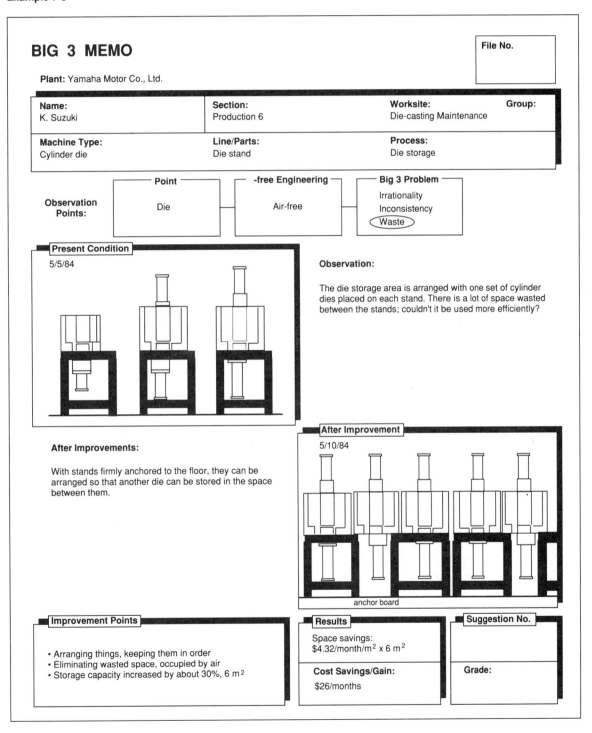

BIG 3 MEMO

File No.

Plant: Yamaha Motor Co., Ltd.

Name: K. Suzuki	**Section:** Production 6	**Worksite:** Die-casting Maintenance	**Group:**
Machine Type: Cylinder die	**Line/Parts:** Die stand	**Process:** Die storage	

Observation Points:

┌─ **Point** ─┐   ┌─ **-free Engineering** ─┐   ┌─ **Big 3 Problem** ─┐
│   Die   │   │   Air-free   │   │ Irrationality   │
│   │   │   │   │ Inconsistency   │
└────────────┘   └─────────────────────────┘   │ (Waste)   │
                                                 └──────────────────────┘

Present Condition

5/5/84

Observation:

The die storage area is arranged with one set of cylinder dies placed on each stand. There is a lot of space wasted between the stands; couldn't it be used more efficiently?

After Improvements:

With stands firmly anchored to the floor, they can be arranged so that another die can be stored in the space between them.

After Improvement

5/10/84

anchor board

Improvement Points

- Arranging things, keeping them in order
- Eliminating wasted space, occupied by air
- Storage capacity increased by about 30%, 6 m^2

Results

Space savings:
$4.32/month/m^2 x 6 m^2

Cost Savings/Gain:
$26/months

Suggestion No.

Grade:

Example 7-9

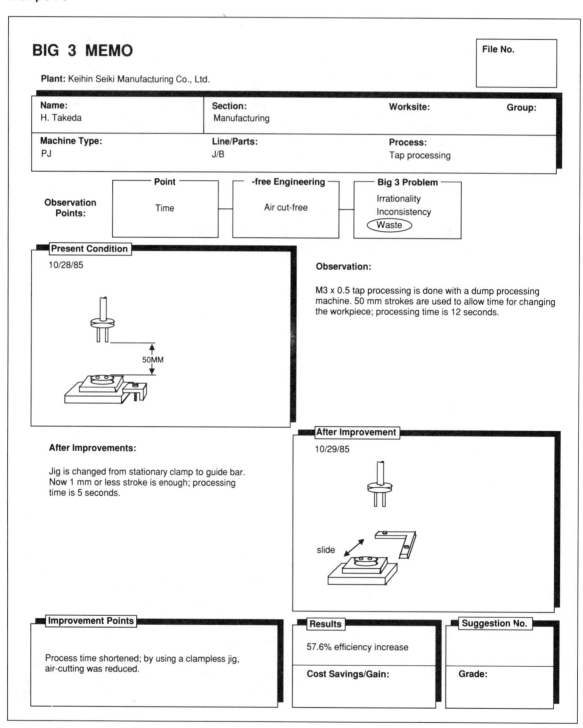

BIG 3 MEMO

File No.

Plant: Keihin Seiki Manufacturing Co., Ltd.

Name: H. Takeda	Section: Manufacturing	Worksite:	Group:
Machine Type: PJ	Line/Parts: J/B	Process: Tap processing	

Observation Points:

Point
Time

-free Engineering
Air cut-free

Big 3 Problem
Irrationality
Inconsistency
Waste

Present Condition

10/28/85

50MM

Observation:

M3 x 0.5 tap processing is done with a dump processing machine. 50 mm strokes are used to allow time for changing the workpiece; processing time is 12 seconds.

After Improvements:

Jig is changed from stationary clamp to guide bar. Now 1 mm or less stroke is enough; processing time is 5 seconds.

After Improvement

10/29/85

slide

Improvement Points

Process time shortened; by using a clampless jig, air-cutting was reduced.

Results

57.6% efficiency increase

Cost Savings/Gain:

Suggestion No.

Grade:

Example 7-10

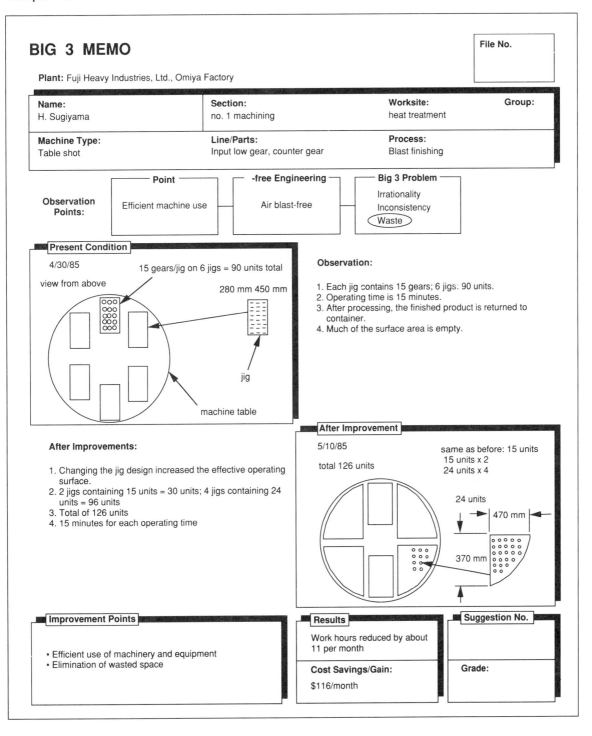

BIG 3 MEMO

File No.

Plant: Fuji Heavy Industries, Ltd., Omiya Factory

Name: H. Sugiyama | **Section:** no. 1 machining | **Worksite:** heat treatment | **Group:**

Machine Type: Table shot | **Line/Parts:** Input low gear, counter gear | **Process:** Blast finishing

Observation Points:

Point — Efficient machine use

-free Engineering — Air blast-free

Big 3 Problem — Irrationality, Inconsistency, (Waste)

Present Condition

4/30/85
view from above
15 gears/jig on 6 jigs = 90 units total
280 mm 450 mm
jig
machine table

Observation:

1. Each jig contains 15 gears; 6 jigs: 90 units.
2. Operating time is 15 minutes.
3. After processing, the finished product is returned to container.
4. Much of the surface area is empty.

After Improvements:

1. Changing the jig design increased the effective operating surface.
2. 2 jigs containing 15 units = 30 units; 4 jigs containing 24 units = 96 units
3. Total of 126 units
4. 15 minutes for each operating time

After Improvement

5/10/85
total 126 units
same as before: 15 units
15 units x 2
24 units x 4
24 units
470 mm
370 mm

Improvement Points

- Efficient use of machinery and equipment
- Elimination of wasted space

Results

Work hours reduced by about 11 per month

Cost Savings/Gain: $116/month

Suggestion No.

Grade:

Example 7 -11

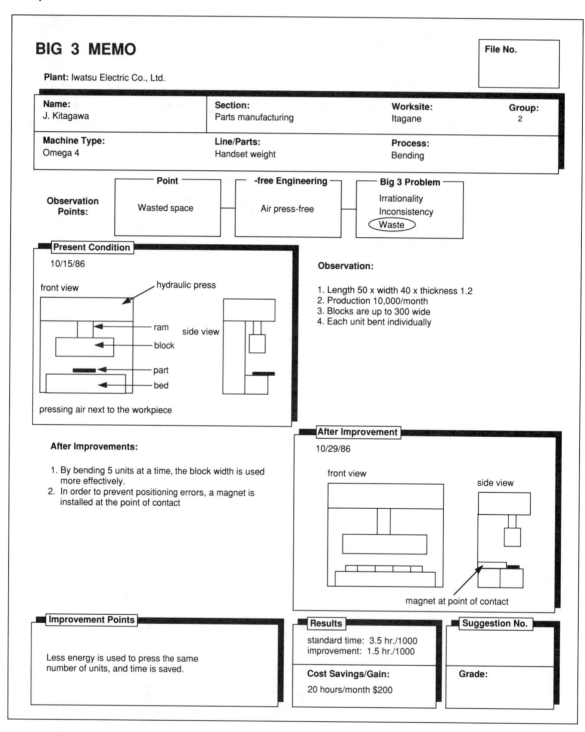

BIG 3 MEMO

Plant: Iwatsu Electric Co., Ltd.

File No.

Name: J. Kitagawa	**Section:** Parts manufacturing	**Worksite:** Itagane	**Group:** 2
Machine Type: Omega 4	**Line/Parts:** Handset weight	**Process:** Bending	

Observation Points:

Point	-free Engineering	Big 3 Problem
Wasted space	Air press-free	Irrationality Inconsistency (Waste)

Present Condition

10/15/86

front view

hydraulic press

ram — block — part — bed — side view

pressing air next to the workpiece

Observation:

1. Length 50 x width 40 x thickness 1.2
2. Production 10,000/month
3. Blocks are up to 300 wide
4. Each unit bent individually

After Improvements:

1. By bending 5 units at a time, the block width is used more effectively.
2. In order to prevent positioning errors, a magnet is installed at the point of contact

After Improvement

10/29/86

front view

side view

magnet at point of contact

Improvement Points

Less energy is used to press the same number of units, and time is saved.

Results

standard time: 3.5 hr./1000
improvement: 1.5 hr./1000

Cost Savings/Gain:

20 hours/month $200

Suggestion No.

Grade:

Example 7-12

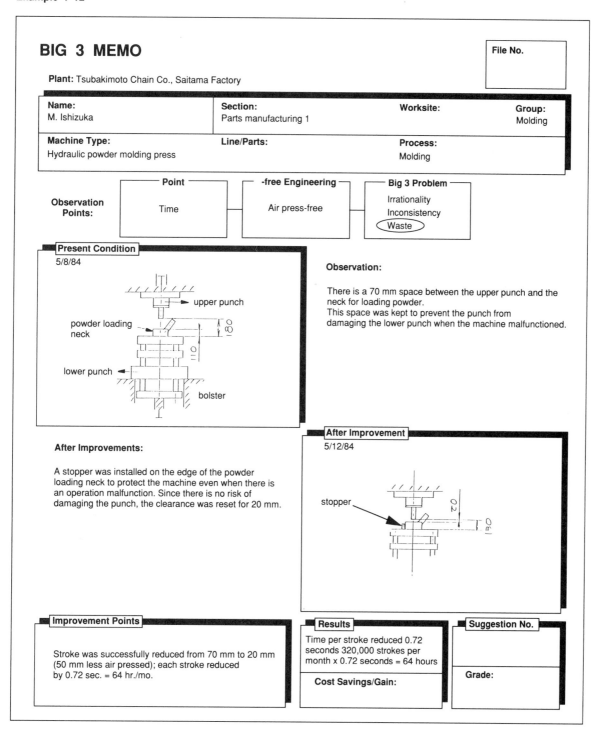

BIG 3 MEMO

File No.

Plant: Tsubakimoto Chain Co., Saitama Factory

| **Name:** M. Ishizuka | **Section:** Parts manufacturing 1 | **Worksite:** | **Group:** Molding |

| **Machine Type:** Hydraulic powder molding press | **Line/Parts:** | **Process:** Molding |

Observation Points:

Point — Time — **-free Engineering** — Air press-free — **Big 3 Problem** — Irrationality / Inconsistency / Waste

Present Condition

5/8/84

upper punch
powder loading neck
lower punch
bolster

Observation:

There is a 70 mm space between the upper punch and the neck for loading powder.
This space was kept to prevent the punch from damaging the lower punch when the machine malfunctioned.

After Improvements:

A stopper was installed on the edge of the powder loading neck to protect the machine even when there is an operation malfunction. Since there is no risk of damaging the punch, the clearance was reset for 20 mm.

After Improvement

5/12/84

stopper

Improvement Points

Stroke was successfully reduced from 70 mm to 20 mm (50 mm less air pressed); each stroke reduced by 0.72 sec. = 64 hr./mo.

Results

Time per stroke reduced 0.72 seconds 320,000 strokes per month x 0.72 seconds = 64 hours

Cost Savings/Gain:

Suggestion No.

Grade:

Example 7-13

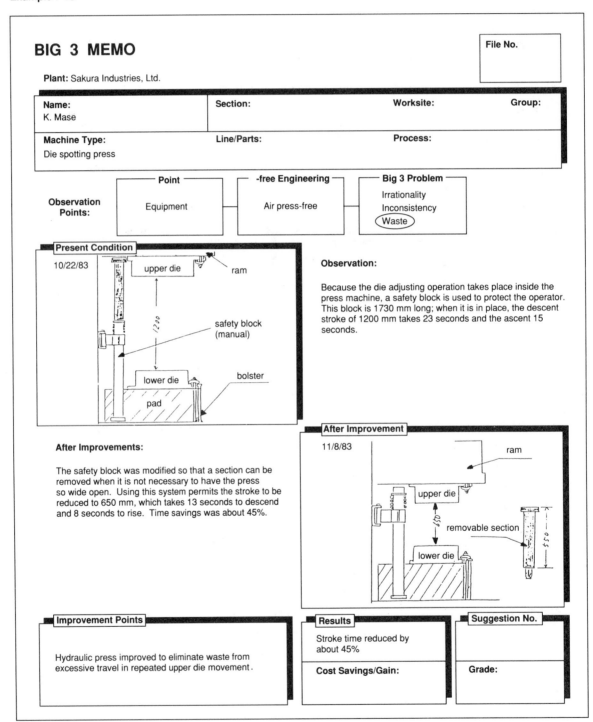

BIG 3 MEMO

File No.

Plant: Sakura Industries, Ltd.

Name: K. Mase	**Section:**	**Worksite:**	**Group:**
Machine Type: Die spotting press	**Line/Parts:**	**Process:**	

Observation Points:

⎡ Point ⎤	⎡ -free Engineering ⎤	⎡ Big 3 Problem ⎤
Equipment	Air press-free	Irrationality Inconsistency (Waste)

Present Condition

10/22/83

upper die — ram

1200

safety block (manual)

lower die — bolster

pad

Observation:

Because the die adjusting operation takes place inside the press machine, a safety block is used to protect the operator. This block is 1730 mm long; when it is in place, the descent stroke of 1200 mm takes 23 seconds and the ascent 15 seconds.

After Improvements:

The safety block was modified so that a section can be removed when it is not necessary to have the press so wide open. Using this system permits the stroke to be reduced to 650 mm, which takes 13 seconds to descend and 8 seconds to rise. Time savings was about 45%.

After Improvement

11/8/83   ram

upper die

650   removable section   550

lower die

Improvement Points

Hydraulic press improved to eliminate waste from excessive travel in repeated upper die movement.

Results

Stroke time reduced by about 45%

Cost Savings/Gain:

Suggestion No.

Grade:

Example 7-14

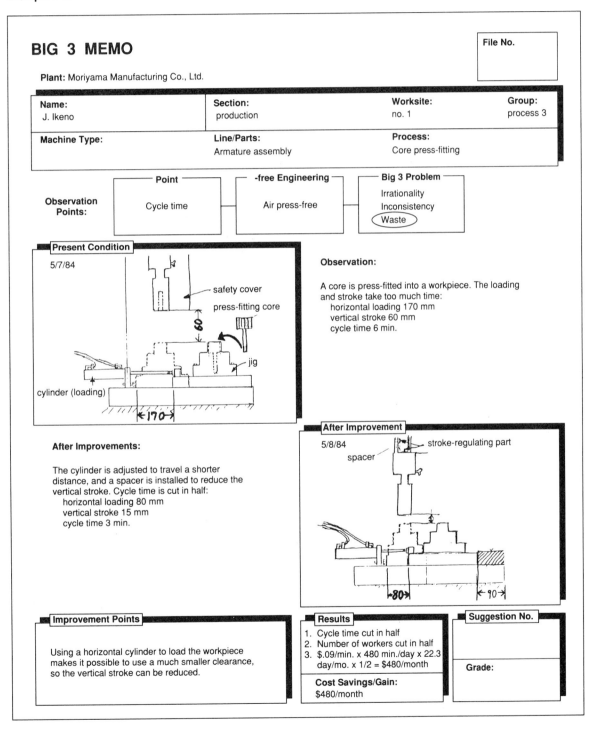

BIG 3 MEMO

File No.

Plant: Moriyama Manufacturing Co., Ltd.

Name: J. Ikeno	**Section:** production	**Worksite:** no. 1	**Group:** process 3

Machine Type:	**Line/Parts:** Armature assembly	**Process:** Core press-fitting

Observation Points:

Point	**-free Engineering**	**Big 3 Problem**
Cycle time	Air press-free	Irrationality Inconsistency Waste

Present Condition

5/7/84

safety cover
press-fitting core
60
jig
cylinder (loading)
170

Observation:

A core is press-fitted into a workpiece. The loading and stroke take too much time:
horizontal loading 170 mm
vertical stroke 60 mm
cycle time 6 min.

After Improvements:

The cylinder is adjusted to travel a shorter distance, and a spacer is installed to reduce the vertical stroke. Cycle time is cut in half:
horizontal loading 80 mm
vertical stroke 15 mm
cycle time 3 min.

After Improvement

5/8/84   stroke-regulating part
spacer
80   90

Improvement Points

Using a horizontal cylinder to load the workpiece makes it possible to use a much smaller clearance, so the vertical stroke can be reduced.

Results

1. Cycle time cut in half
2. Number of workers cut in half
3. $.09/min. x 480 min./day x 22.3 day/mo. x 1/2 = $480/month

Cost Savings/Gain:
$480/month

Suggestion No.

Grade:

Example 7-15

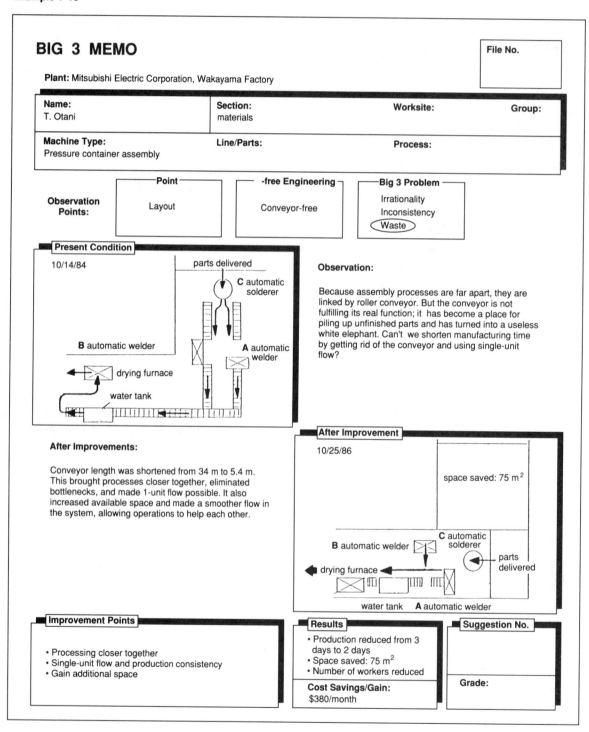

BIG 3 MEMO

File No.

Plant: Mitsubishi Electric Corporation, Wakayama Factory

| **Name:** T. Otani | **Section:** materials | **Worksite:** | **Group:** |
| **Machine Type:** Pressure container assembly | **Line/Parts:** | **Process:** |

Observation Points:

| ┌ Point ┐ Layout | ┌ -free Engineering ┐ Conveyor-free | ┌ Big 3 Problem ┐ Irrationality Inconsistency Waste |

Present Condition

10/14/84

parts delivered

C automatic solderer

B automatic welder

A automatic welder

drying furnace

water tank

Observation:

Because assembly processes are far apart, they are linked by roller conveyor. But the conveyor is not fulfilling its real function; it has become a place for piling up unfinished parts and has turned into a useless white elephant. Can't we shorten manufacturing time by getting rid of the conveyor and using single-unit flow?

After Improvements:

Conveyor length was shortened from 34 m to 5.4 m. This brought processes closer together, eliminated bottlenecks, and made 1-unit flow possible. It also increased available space and made a smoother flow in the system, allowing operations to help each other.

After Improvement

10/25/86

space saved: 75 m^2

B automatic welder

C automatic solderer

parts delivered

drying furnace

water tank   A automatic welder

Improvement Points

• Processing closer together
• Single-unit flow and production consistency
• Gain additional space

Results

• Production reduced from 3 days to 2 days
• Space saved: 75 m^2
• Number of workers reduced

Cost Savings/Gain: $380/month

Suggestion No.

Grade:

Example 7-16

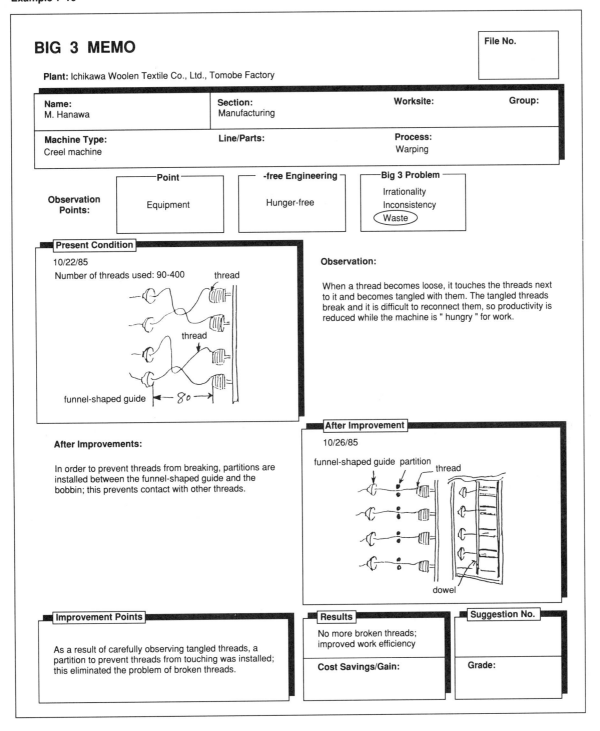

BIG 3 MEMO   File No.

Plant: Ichikawa Woolen Textile Co., Ltd., Tomobe Factory

Name: M. Hanawa	**Section:** Manufacturing	**Worksite:**	**Group:**
Machine Type: Creel machine	**Line/Parts:**	**Process:** Warping	

Observation Points:

- Point: Equipment
- -free Engineering: Hunger-free
- Big 3 Problem: Irrationality / Inconsistency / (Waste)

Present Condition

10/22/85
Number of threads used: 90-400

thread
thread
funnel-shaped guide ⊢— 80 —

Observation:

When a thread becomes loose, it touches the threads next to it and becomes tangled with them. The tangled threads break and it is difficult to reconnect them, so productivity is reduced while the machine is " hungry " for work.

After Improvements:

In order to prevent threads from breaking, partitions are installed between the funnel-shaped guide and the bobbin; this prevents contact with other threads.

After Improvement

10/26/85
funnel-shaped guide partition   thread

dowel

Improvement Points

As a result of carefully observing tangled threads, a partition to prevent threads from touching was installed; this eliminated the problem of broken threads.

Results

No more broken threads; improved work efficiency

Cost Savings/Gain:

Suggestion No.

Grade:

Example 7-17

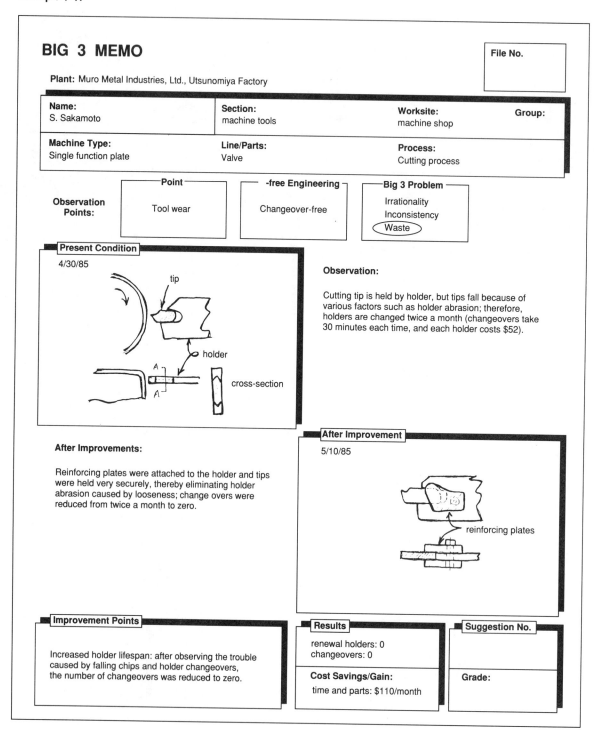

BIG 3 MEMO

File No.

Plant: Muro Metal Industries, Ltd., Utsunomiya Factory

Name: S. Sakamoto	**Section:** machine tools	**Worksite:** machine shop	**Group:**
Machine Type: Single function plate	**Line/Parts:** Valve	**Process:** Cutting process	

Observation Points:

┌─ **Point** ─┐ ┌─ **-free Engineering** ─┐ ┌─ **Big 3 Problem** ─┐
Tool wear / Changeover-free / Irrationality / Inconsistency / (Waste)

Present Condition

4/30/85

tip

holder

A

A

cross-section

Observation:

Cutting tip is held by holder, but tips fall because of various factors such as holder abrasion; therefore, holders are changed twice a month (changeovers take 30 minutes each time, and each holder costs $52).

After Improvements:

Reinforcing plates were attached to the holder and tips were held very securely, thereby eliminating holder abrasion caused by looseness; change overs were reduced from twice a month to zero.

After Improvement

5/10/85

reinforcing plates

Improvement Points

Increased holder lifespan: after observing the trouble caused by falling chips and holder changeovers, the number of changeovers was reduced to zero.

Results

renewal holders: 0
changeovers: 0

Cost Savings/Gain:

time and parts: $110/month

Suggestion No.

Grade:

Example 7-18

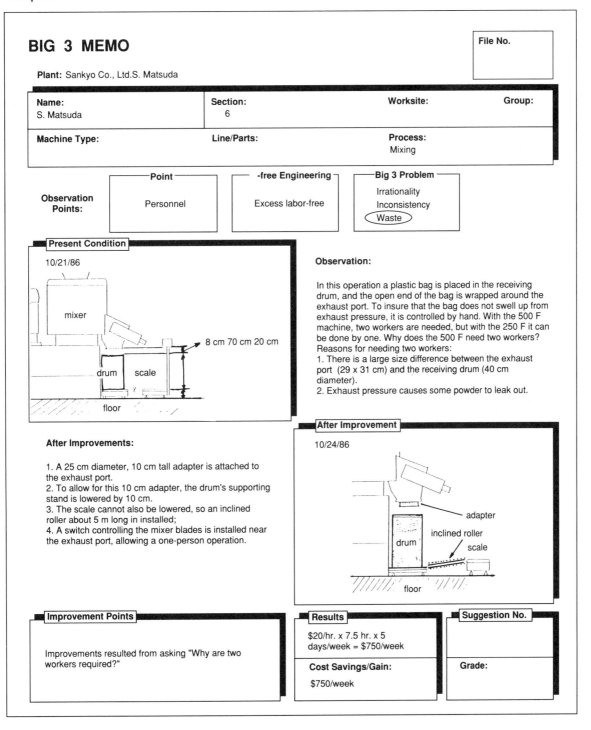

BIG 3 MEMO

File No.

Plant: Sankyo Co., Ltd.S. Matsuda

| Name:
S. Matsuda | Section:
6 | Worksite: | Group: |

| Machine Type: | Line/Parts: | Process:
Mixing |

Observation Points:

┌─ Point ─┐
Personnel

┌─ -free Engineering ─┐
Excess labor-free

┌─ Big 3 Problem ─┐
Irrationality
Inconsistency
(Waste)

■ Present Condition

10/21/86

mixer

drum   scale

floor

8 cm 70 cm 20 cm

Observation:

In this operation a plastic bag is placed in the receiving drum, and the open end of the bag is wrapped around the exhaust port. To insure that the bag does not swell up from exhaust pressure, it is controlled by hand. With the 500 F machine, two workers are needed, but with the 250 F it can be done by one. Why does the 500 F need two workers? Reasons for needing two workers:
1. There is a large size difference between the exhaust port (29 x 31 cm) and the receiving drum (40 cm diameter).
2. Exhaust pressure causes some powder to leak out.

After Improvements:

1. A 25 cm diameter, 10 cm tall adapter is attached to the exhaust port.
2. To allow for this 10 cm adapter, the drum's supporting stand is lowered by 10 cm.
3. The scale cannot also be lowered, so an inclined roller about 5 m long in installed;
4. A switch controlling the mixer blades is installed near the exhaust port, allowing a one-person operation.

■ After Improvement

10/24/86

adapter
inclined roller
drum
scale
floor

■ Improvement Points

Improvements resulted from asking "Why are two workers required?"

■ Results

$20/hr. x 7.5 hr. x 5 days/week = $750/week

Cost Savings/Gain:

$750/week

■ Suggestion No.

Grade:

Example 7-19

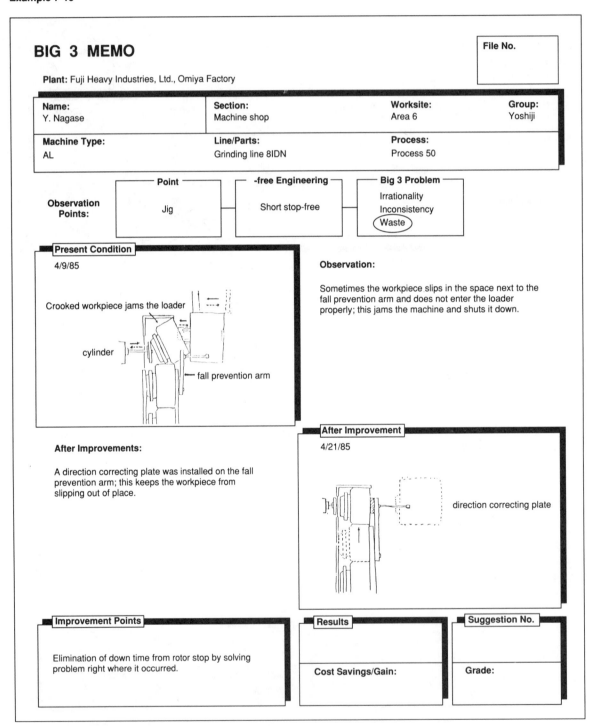

BIG 3 MEMO

File No.

Plant: Fuji Heavy Industries, Ltd., Omiya Factory

Name: Y. Nagase	**Section:** Machine shop	**Worksite:** Area 6	**Group:** Yoshiji
Machine Type: AL	**Line/Parts:** Grinding line 8IDN	**Process:** Process 50	

Observation Points:

─ Point ─	─ -free Engineering ─	─ Big 3 Problem ─
Jig	Short stop-free	Irrationality Inconsistency (Waste)

Present Condition

4/9/85

Crooked workpiece jams the loader

cylinder

fall prevention arm

Observation:

Sometimes the workpiece slips in the space next to the fall prevention arm and does not enter the loader properly; this jams the machine and shuts it down.

After Improvements:

A direction correcting plate was installed on the fall prevention arm; this keeps the workpiece from slipping out of place.

After Improvement

4/21/85

direction correcting plate

Improvement Points

Elimination of down time from rotor stop by solving problem right where it occurred.

Results

Cost Savings/Gain:

Suggestion No.

Grade:

Example 7-20

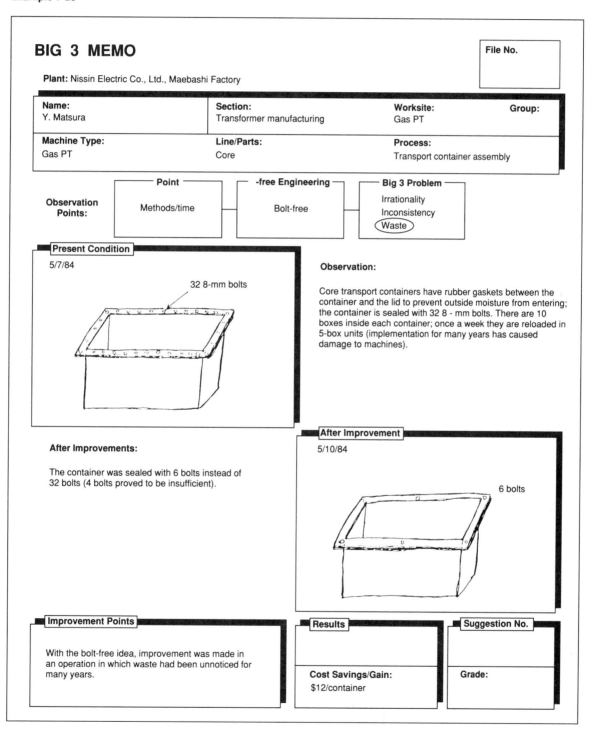

BIG 3 MEMO

File No.

Plant: Nissin Electric Co., Ltd., Maebashi Factory

Name: Y. Matsura	**Section:** Transformer manufacturing	**Worksite:** Gas PT	**Group:**
Machine Type: Gas PT	**Line/Parts:** Core	**Process:** Transport container assembly	

Observation Points:

Point — Methods/time

-free Engineering — Bolt-free

Big 3 Problem — Irrationality / Inconsistency / (Waste)

Present Condition

5/7/84

32 8-mm bolts

Observation:

Core transport containers have rubber gaskets between the container and the lid to prevent outside moisture from entering; the container is sealed with 32 8 - mm bolts. There are 10 boxes inside each container; once a week they are reloaded in 5-box units (implementation for many years has caused damage to machines).

After Improvements:

The container was sealed with 6 bolts instead of 32 bolts (4 bolts proved to be insufficient).

After Improvement

5/10/84

6 bolts

Improvement Points

With the bolt-free idea, improvement was made in an operation in which waste had been unnoticed for many years.

Results

Cost Savings/Gain:
$12/container

Suggestion No.

Grade:

Example 7-21

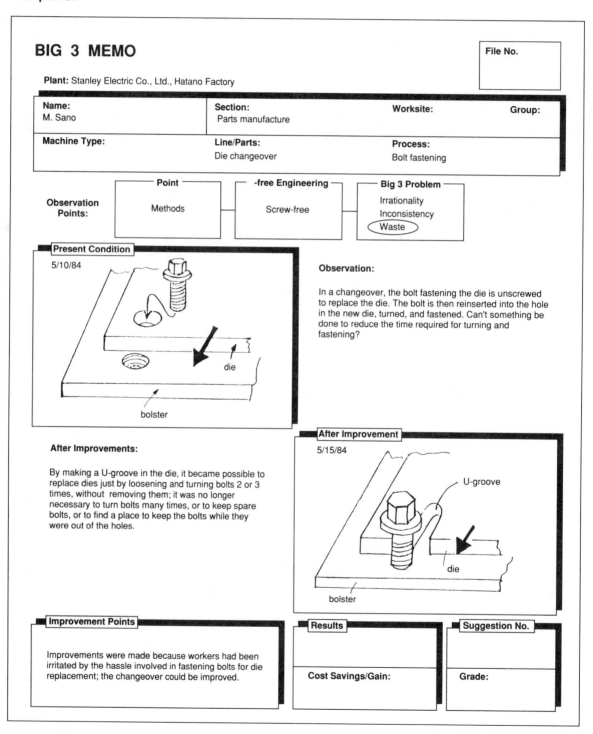

BIG 3 MEMO

File No.

Plant: Stanley Electric Co., Ltd., Hatano Factory

Name: M. Sano	Section: Parts manufacture	Worksite:	Group:
Machine Type:	Line/Parts: Die changeover	Process: Bolt fastening	

Observation Points:

Point	-free Engineering	Big 3 Problem
Methods	Screw-free	Irrationality Inconsistency (Waste)

Present Condition

5/10/84

die

bolster

Observation:

In a changeover, the bolt fastening the die is unscrewed to replace the die. The bolt is then reinserted into the hole in the new die, turned, and fastened. Can't something be done to reduce the time required for turning and fastening?

After Improvements:

By making a U-groove in the die, it became possible to replace dies just by loosening and turning bolts 2 or 3 times, without removing them; it was no longer necessary to turn bolts many times, or to keep spare bolts, or to find a place to keep the bolts while they were out of the holes.

After Improvement

5/15/84

U-groove

die

bolster

Improvement Points

Improvements were made because workers had been irritated by the hassle involved in fastening bolts for die replacement; the changeover could be improved.

Results

Cost Savings/Gain:

Suggestion No.

Grade:

Example 7-22

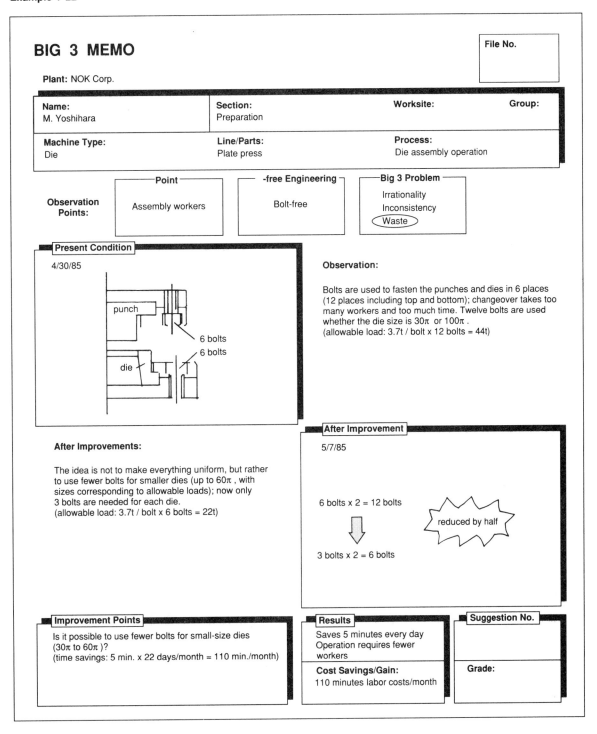

BIG 3 MEMO

File No.

Plant: NOK Corp.

Name: M. Yoshihara	**Section:** Preparation	**Worksite:**	**Group:**
Machine Type: Die	**Line/Parts:** Plate press	**Process:** Die assembly operation	

Observation Points:

┌─ **Point** ─┐
Assembly workers

┌─ **-free Engineering** ─┐
Bolt-free

┌─ **Big 3 Problem** ─┐
Irrationality
Inconsistency
⟨Waste⟩

Present Condition

4/30/85

punch

6 bolts
6 bolts

die

Observation:

Bolts are used to fasten the punches and dies in 6 places (12 places including top and bottom); changeover takes too many workers and too much time. Twelve bolts are used whether the die size is 30π or 100π.
(allowable load: 3.7t / bolt x 12 bolts = 44t)

After Improvements:

The idea is not to make everything uniform, but rather to use fewer bolts for smaller dies (up to 60π, with sizes corresponding to allowable loads); now only 3 bolts are needed for each die.
(allowable load: 3.7t / bolt x 6 bolts = 22t)

After Improvement

5/7/85

6 bolts x 2 = 12 bolts

⬇

3 bolts x 2 = 6 bolts

✦ reduced by half ✦

Improvement Points

Is it possible to use fewer bolts for small-size dies (30π to 60π)?
(time savings: 5 min. x 22 days/month = 110 min./month)

Results

Saves 5 minutes every day
Operation requires fewer workers

Cost Savings/Gain:
110 minutes labor costs/month

Suggestion No.

Grade:

Example 7-23

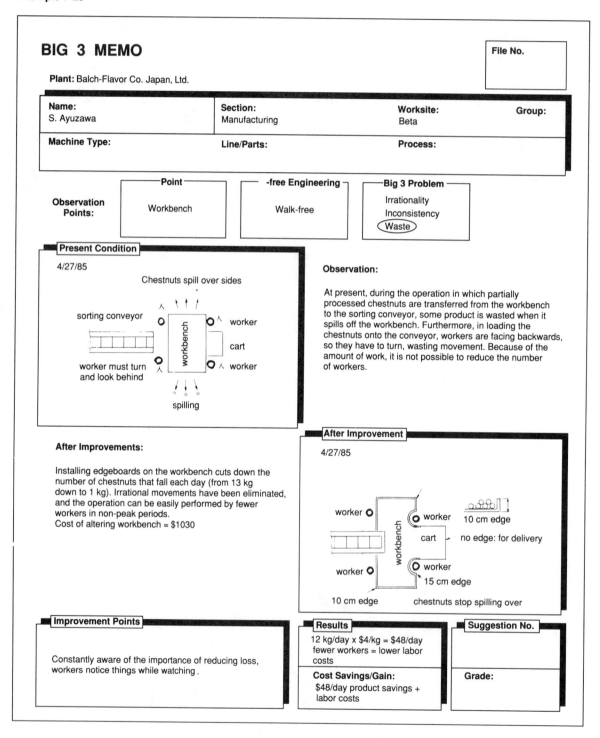

BIG 3 MEMO

File No.

Plant: Balch-Flavor Co. Japan, Ltd.

Name: S. Ayuzawa	**Section:** Manufacturing	**Worksite:** Beta	**Group:**
Machine Type:	**Line/Parts:**	**Process:**	

Observation Points:

⌐ Point ⌐	⌐ -free Engineering ⌐	⌐ Big 3 Problem ⌐
Workbench	Walk-free	Irrationality Inconsistency (Waste)

▮ Present Condition

4/27/85

Chestnuts spill over sides

sorting conveyor

worker

workbench

cart

worker

worker must turn
and look behind

worker

spilling

Observation:

At present, during the operation in which partially processed chestnuts are transferred from the workbench to the sorting conveyor, some product is wasted when it spills off the workbench. Furthermore, in loading the chestnuts onto the conveyor, workers are facing backwards, so they have to turn, wasting movement. Because of the amount of work, it is not possible to reduce the number of workers.

After Improvements:

Installing edgeboards on the workbench cuts down the number of chestnuts that fall each day (from 13 kg down to 1 kg). Irrational movements have been eliminated, and the operation can be easily performed by fewer workers in non-peak periods.
Cost of altering workbench = $1030

▮ After Improvement

4/27/85

worker

worker

10 cm edge

workbench

cart · no edge: for delivery

worker

worker

15 cm edge

10 cm edge   chestnuts stop spilling over

▮ Improvement Points

Constantly aware of the importance of reducing loss, workers notice things while watching .

▮ Results

12 kg/day x $4/kg = $48/day
fewer workers = lower labor costs

Cost Savings/Gain:
$48/day product savings + labor costs

▮ Suggestion No.

Grade:

Example 7-24

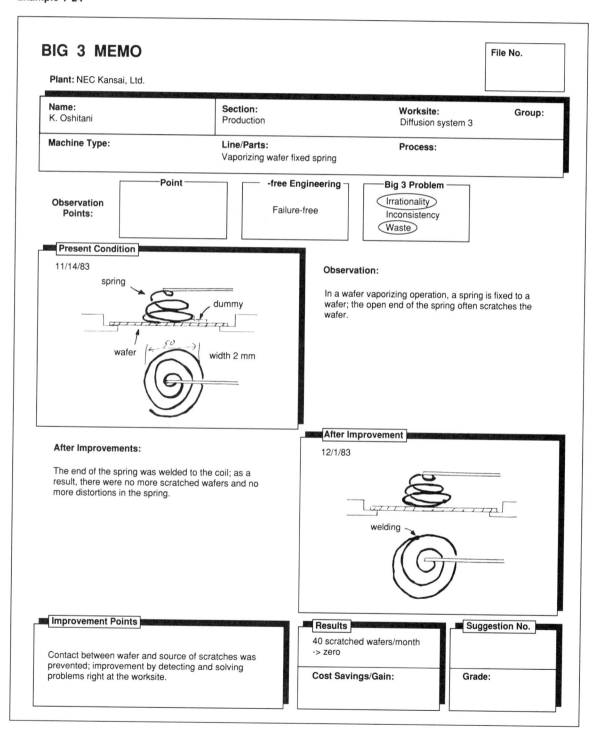

BIG 3 MEMO

File No.

Plant: NEC Kansai, Ltd.

Name: K. Oshitani	Section: Production	Worksite: Diffusion system 3	Group:
Machine Type:	Line/Parts: Vaporizing wafer fixed spring	Process:	

Observation Points:

┌─ Point ─┐

┌─ -free Engineering ─┐
Failure-free

┌─ Big 3 Problem ─┐
(Irrationality)
Inconsistency
(Waste)

Present Condition

11/14/83

spring
dummy
wafer
width 2 mm

Observation:

In a wafer vaporizing operation, a spring is fixed to a wafer; the open end of the spring often scratches the wafer.

After Improvements:

The end of the spring was welded to the coil; as a result, there were no more scratched wafers and no more distortions in the spring.

After Improvement

12/1/83

welding

Improvement Points

Contact between wafer and source of scratches was prevented; improvement by detecting and solving problems right at the worksite.

Results

40 scratched wafers/month
-> zero

Cost Savings/Gain:

Suggestion No.

Grade:

Example 7-25

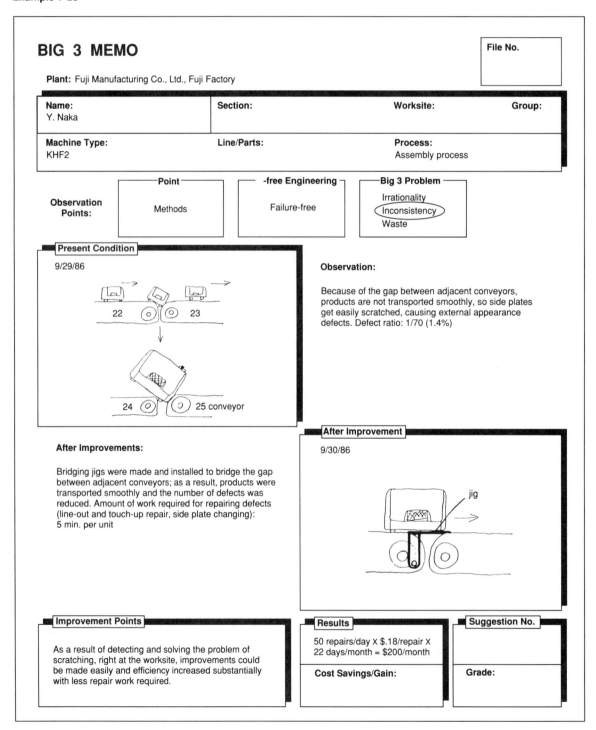

BIG 3 MEMO

File No.

Plant: Fuji Manufacturing Co., Ltd., Fuji Factory

Name:
Y. Naka

Section:

Worksite:

Group:

Machine Type:
KHF2

Line/Parts:

Process:
Assembly process

Observation Points:

┌─── Point ───┐
Methods

┌─── -free Engineering ───┐
Failure-free

┌─── Big 3 Problem ───┐
Irrationality
(Inconsistency)
Waste

Present Condition

9/29/86

22   23

24   25 conveyor

Observation:

Because of the gap between adjacent conveyors, products are not transported smoothly, so side plates get easily scratched, causing external appearance defects. Defect ratio: 1/70 (1.4%)

After Improvements:

Bridging jigs were made and installed to bridge the gap between adjacent conveyors; as a result, products were transported smoothly and the number of defects was reduced. Amount of work required for repairing defects (line-out and touch-up repair, side plate changing): 5 min. per unit

After Improvement

9/30/86

jig

Improvement Points

As a result of detecting and solving the problem of scratching, right at the worksite, improvements could be made easily and efficiency increased substantially with less repair work required.

Results

50 repairs/day X $.18/repair X
22 days/month = $200/month

Cost Savings/Gain:

Suggestion No.

Grade:

Example 7-26

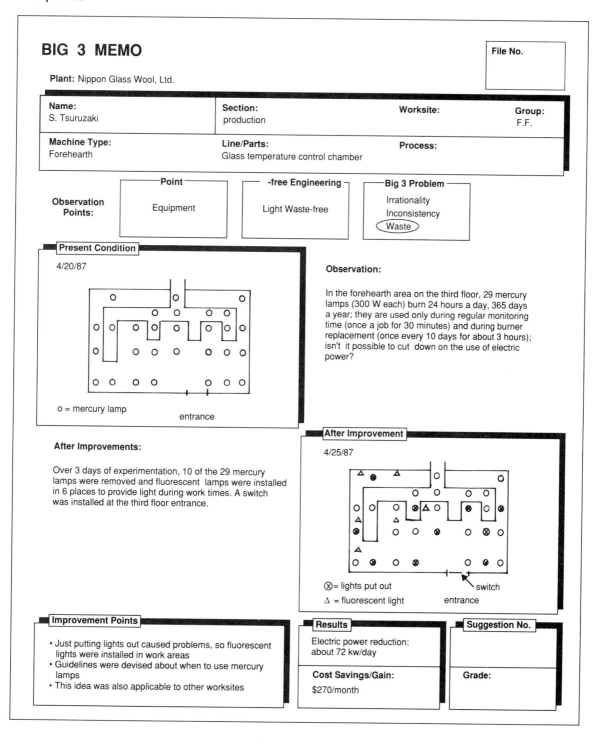

BIG 3 MEMO

File No.

Plant: Nippon Glass Wool, Ltd.

| **Name:** S. Tsuruzaki | **Section:** production | **Worksite:** | **Group:** F.F. |

| **Machine Type:** Forehearth | **Line/Parts:** Glass temperature control chamber | **Process:** |

Observation Points:

- Point — Equipment
- -free Engineering — Light Waste-free
- Big 3 Problem — Irrationality / Inconsistency / (Waste)

Present Condition

4/20/87

o = mercury lamp

entrance

Observation:

In the forehearth area on the third floor, 29 mercury lamps (300 W each) burn 24 hours a day, 365 days a year; they are used only during regular monitoring time (once a job for 30 minutes) and during burner replacement (once every 10 days for about 3 hours); isn't it possible to cut down on the use of electric power?

After Improvements:

Over 3 days of experimentation, 10 of the 29 mercury lamps were removed and fluorescent lamps were installed in 6 places to provide light during work times. A switch was installed at the third floor entrance.

After Improvement

4/25/87

⊗ = lights put out

Δ = fluorescent light

switch

entrance

Improvement Points

- Just putting lights out caused problems, so fluorescent lights were installed in work areas
- Guidelines were devised about when to use mercury lamps
- This idea was also applicable to other worksites

Results

Electric power reduction: about 72 kw/day

Cost Savings/Gain: $270/month

Suggestion No.

Grade:

Example 7-27

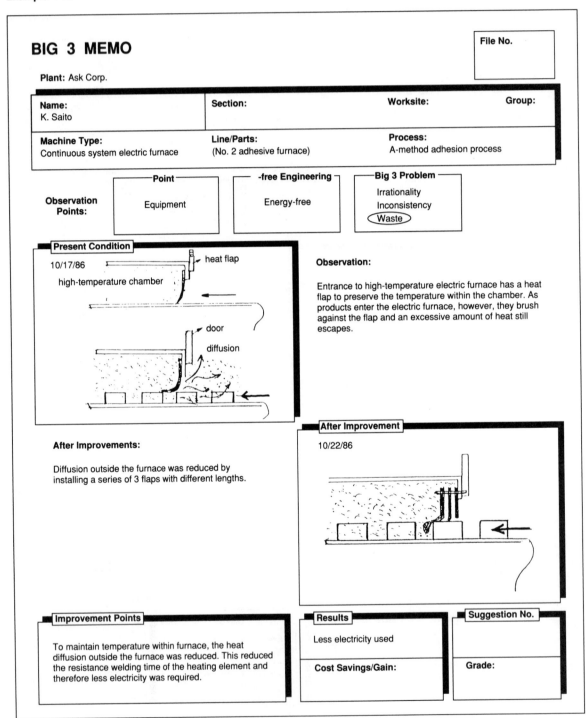

BIG 3 MEMO

File No.

Plant: Ask Corp.

Name: K. Saito	Section:	Worksite:	Group:

Machine Type: Continuous system electric furnace	Line/Parts: (No. 2 adhesive furnace)	Process: A-method adhesion process

Observation Points:

┌─ Point ─┐
Equipment

┌─ -free Engineering ─┐
Energy-free

┌─ Big 3 Problem ─┐
Irrationality
Inconsistency
(Waste)

Present Condition

10/17/86

high-temperature chamber

heat flap

door

diffusion

Observation:

Entrance to high-temperature electric furnace has a heat flap to preserve the temperature within the chamber. As products enter the electric furnace, however, they brush against the flap and an excessive amount of heat still escapes.

After Improvements:

Diffusion outside the furnace was reduced by installing a series of 3 flaps with different lengths.

After Improvement

10/22/86

Improvement Points

To maintain temperature within furnace, the heat diffusion outside the furnace was reduced. This reduced the resistance welding time of the heating element and therefore less electricity was required.

Results

Less electricity used

Cost Savings/Gain:

Suggestion No.

Grade:

Example 7-28

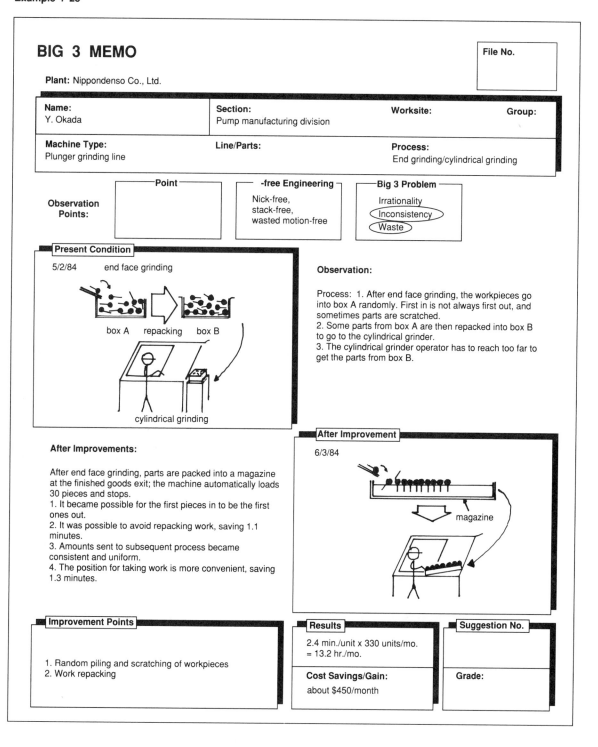

BIG 3 MEMO

File No.

Plant: Nippondenso Co., Ltd.

| **Name:** Y. Okada | **Section:** Pump manufacturing division | **Worksite:** | **Group:** |

| **Machine Type:** Plunger grinding line | **Line/Parts:** | **Process:** End grinding/cylindrical grinding |

Observation Points:

Point

-free Engineering
Nick-free,
stack-free,
wasted motion-free

Big 3 Problem
Irrationality
Inconsistency
Waste

Present Condition

5/2/84   end face grinding

box A   repacking   box B

cylindrical grinding

Observation:

Process: 1. After end face grinding, the workpieces go into box A randomly. First in is not always first out, and sometimes parts are scratched.
2. Some parts from box A are then repacked into box B to go to the cylindrical grinder.
3. The cylindrical grinder operator has to reach too far to get the parts from box B.

After Improvements:

After end face grinding, parts are packed into a magazine at the finished goods exit; the machine automatically loads 30 pieces and stops.
1. It became possible for the first pieces in to be the first ones out.
2. It was possible to avoid repacking work, saving 1.1 minutes.
3. Amounts sent to subsequent process became consistent and uniform.
4. The position for taking work is more convenient, saving 1.3 minutes.

After Improvement

6/3/84

magazine

Improvement Points

1. Random piling and scratching of workpieces
2. Work repacking

Results

2.4 min./unit x 330 units/mo.
= 13.2 hr./mo.

Cost Savings/Gain:

about $450/month

Suggestion No.

Grade:

Example 7-29

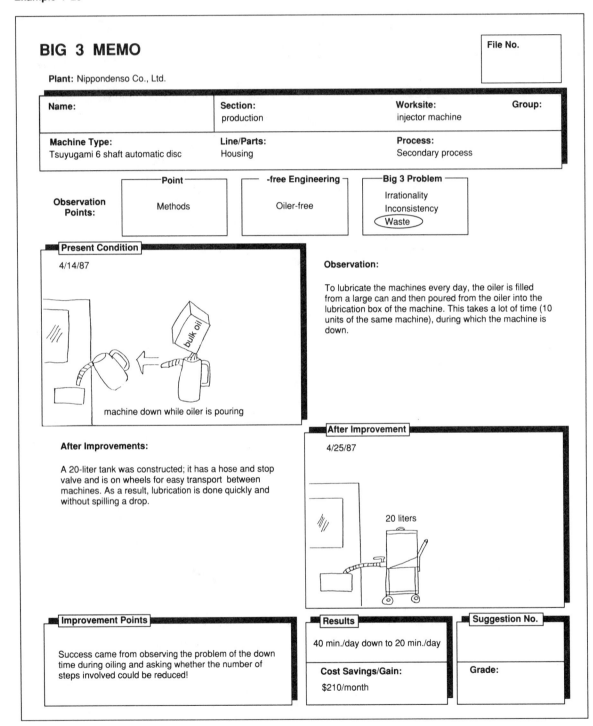

BIG 3 MEMO

File No.

Plant: Nippondenso Co., Ltd.

Name:	**Section:** production	**Worksite:** injector machine	**Group:**
Machine Type: Tsuyugami 6 shaft automatic disc	**Line/Parts:** Housing	**Process:** Secondary process	

Observation Points:

Point — Methods

-free Engineering — Oiler-free

Big 3 Problem —
Irrationality
Inconsistency
Waste

Present Condition

4/14/87

bulk oil

machine down while oiler is pouring

Observation:

To lubricate the machines every day, the oiler is filled from a large can and then poured from the oiler into the lubrication box of the machine. This takes a lot of time (10 units of the same machine), during which the machine is down.

After Improvements:

A 20-liter tank was constructed; it has a hose and stop valve and is on wheels for easy transport between machines. As a result, lubrication is done quickly and without spilling a drop.

After Improvement

4/25/87

20 liters

Improvement Points

Success came from observing the problem of the down time during oiling and asking whether the number of steps involved could be reduced!

Results

40 min./day down to 20 min./day

Cost Savings/Gain:
$210/month

Suggestion No.

Grade:

Example 7-30

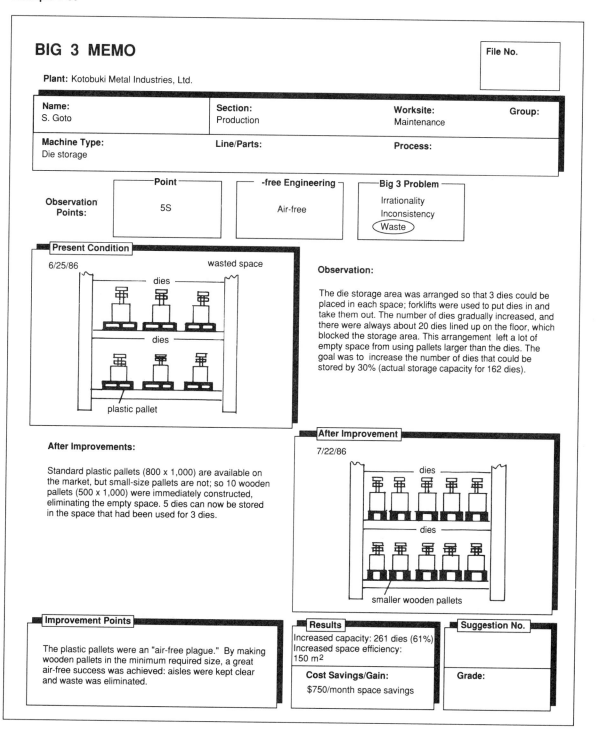

BIG 3 MEMO

File No.

Plant: Kotobuki Metal Industries, Ltd.

Name: S. Goto	**Section:** Production	**Worksite:** Maintenance	**Group:**
Machine Type: Die storage	**Line/Parts:**	**Process:**	

Observation Points:

—— Point —— 5S	— -free Engineering — Air-free	— Big 3 Problem — Irrationality Inconsistency (Waste)

Present Condition

6/25/86   wasted space

dies

dies

plastic pallet

Observation:

The die storage area was arranged so that 3 dies could be placed in each space; forklifts were used to put dies in and take them out. The number of dies gradually increased, and there were always about 20 dies lined up on the floor, which blocked the storage area. This arrangement left a lot of empty space from using pallets larger than the dies. The goal was to increase the number of dies that could be stored by 30% (actual storage capacity for 162 dies).

After Improvements:

Standard plastic pallets (800 x 1,000) are available on the market, but small-size pallets are not; so 10 wooden pallets (500 x 1,000) were immediately constructed, eliminating the empty space. 5 dies can now be stored in the space that had been used for 3 dies.

After Improvement

7/22/86

dies

dies

smaller wooden pallets

Improvement Points

The plastic pallets were an "air-free plague." By making wooden pallets in the minimum required size, a great air-free success was achieved: aisles were kept clear and waste was eliminated.

Results

Increased capacity: 261 dies (61%)
Increased space efficiency:
150 m^2

Cost Savings/Gain:

$750/month space savings

Suggestion No.

Grade:

CHAPTER 8

Practical Tips for Using the Big 3 Memo to Create the Problem-free Workplace

After introducing the idea of problem-free engineering throughout the company, you can start an improvement program for detecting and solving problems using the Big 3 Memo. The information recorded on the memo form becomes the basis for continual improvement activities.

A method as simple as this should be easy to establish but as a practical matter, it takes some effort and commitment to get any improvement program running smoothly on its own. Our effort at Yamaha took years of trial and error. I sometimes was reminded of the difficulties of beginning a new religion. I was born in the Year of the Tiger, however, and seem to have the tenacity attributed to such people.

In my case, I was fortunate to lead the improvement support group for the Yamaha Motor best line foremen. These people agreed with my ideas and helped to put them into practice. People like these give you a double advantage: They produce solid results.

Results are an important key to gaining support for a Big 3 Memo program. People are not convinced when you say, "By doing this and that, you should get such and such results." But it's hard for people to criticize when you can say, "By doing this and that, we *actually got* such and such results."

Producing actual results is the only way to overcome employee resistance — criticism and excuses for not supporting or participating in the program. We reflected constantly on our successes as well as on occasional failures, taking everything as a potentially valuable experience. This chapter draws on some of these experiences to illustrate how these methods work successfully.

The Big 3 Memo Helps Other Improvement Activities

When workers begin to write up Big 3 Memos, they may object: "Oh no, not another improvement system. We already have a Total Quality Control program, as well as Total Productive Maintenance (TPM) and other improvement activities."

My answer to this objection is that using the memo form will help each person in the company better carry out these other activities. Machine maintenance and quality assurance often can be improved through observation and creative use of the memo. Use of the Big 3 Memo can be combined effectively with any other improvement activity.

In fact, if a company skillfully performs TPM, that company's success also is involved with Total Quality Control (TQC) activities as well as Total Industrial Engineering (TIE, a company-wide rationalization program). These kinds of activities cannot be challenged.

Some people may be uncomfortable about using the Big 3 Memo form, believing it is too complicated. I remind them that people at work jot down notes and memos all the time about various situations. The Big 3 Memo notebook simply provides a convenient way to preserve and organize memos about things that might be improved.

Producing Results to Convince Top Management

Over the years, I have conducted many workshops and seminars for foremen and their supervisors on problem-free engineering and the Big 3 Memo. My priority was to train those likely to show the best results, and then to use those results to convince upper management of the value of the program.

Workshop participants are always excited about what they learn. They often write in their evaluations things like "I learned the knack of detecting waste," "I never knew this much waste was involved," "This is really suitable for on-site improvement activities," or "We must keep going and make more progress." But when they return to their jobs, they often have trouble keeping these ideas alive and producing the results that will persuade top management to adopt a Big 3 Memo program. Usually one of the following things happens:

1. Management-level people approve the program based on their own experience and start it up through their subordinates one after another.
2. Improvement staff members participate in seminars and become completely aligned with the ideas involved. They then

form information groups, persuade their managers and others whose approval is needed, and begin a campaign to spread the ideas throughout the appropriate divisions.

3. Supervisors attend the seminar and believe their participation was valuable, but they can't convince their superiors that the program is beneficial, so they start their own activities by themselves, without management involvement.

4. People who attended the seminar don't start up any Big 3 Memo activities because their superiors show no interest or support.

5. Supervisors who attended the program think it's a lot of bother to carry out these activities and don't even try to get an improvement program going.

After considering many situations like these, we can generalize that companies in situations 1 and 2 can get a program going relatively smoothly. Companies in situations 3 and 4, though unfortunately more numerous, have a harder time of it. The fifth situation is really inexcusable and raises doubts about whether the people should be supervisors. It is important, therefore, to motivate people in top management or the appropriate supervisors.

Naturally, some environments simply cannot be changed by seminar participants. But if they believe their own experiences were valuable, they go back and start using and promoting problem-free engineering in their own work areas. The key is to first contribute their own performance and produce actual results. To educate and convince upper management of the significance of a Big 3 Memo program, they have to express a passionate commitment through their own efforts.

Administering the Program

Administering the program does not require an extremely sweeping organizational change. It can be adequately accomplished as a supplementary project. Since demonstrating cost savings is a key to the value of the program, it is useful to create an administrative system to keep track of the data and calculate the results.

At present the Big 3 Memo system is in the pilot stage at many companies, which tend to create administrative structures to fit the situation rather than any set form. It would be ideal, of course, to have a special Big 3 Memo office. In fact the companies using these programs most successfully have created distinct offices to run them. In companies where the program has not achieved full status, it is carried out as a supplementary activity of the improvement proposal system or TPM office.

The following situations were found in some of the successful companies:

- Enthusiastic and committed promotional staff members
- A system for administering the program, such as
  - The improvement suggestion office
  - A TQC office, incorporating the Memo into TQC activities
  - A TPM office that handles the Memo reporting and calculations within the TPM evaluation standards
  - Incorporating the Big 3 Memo in TIE leader training
- Monthly reports on number of new memos, number of solutions, and cost savings posted in the workplace or in meeting areas. This usually gets the attention of the relevant managers and administrative people, giving them a solid grasp of the results.
- A Big 3 Memo committee, with members participating from each section, to promote formation and activities of information exchanges, study groups, and factory visit groups.

In short, the key factors that determine success or failure are clarifying the committee organization and assigning the roles to be played by each person.

Who Should Use the Big 3 Memo?

The ideal situation for problem-free engineering is for every member of the company to participate by keeping Big 3 Memo workbooks. This approach is not always suitable for every situation, however, and it may be best to start with a pilot program with one or more specific groups. My own experience suggests focusing initially on the following approaches, which have the most potential for producing results that will promote the program:

1. First-line supervisors should start using the memo early on because they are in the best position to start raising the efficiency and "problem-consciousness" of the workplace. With training and support, they will become effective leaders for their subordinates. Every job is different, and not every supervisor will be equally enthusiastic about using the memos. But a special effort should be made to get them involved; their participation is crucial to the success of a problem-free workplace program.

2. Each work team should have a copy of the Big 3 Memo workbook. Someone writes up a memo whenever any person notices a problem is noticed. The work team considers these together and works with their supervisor to devise solutions. As employees learn to detect, write up, and solve problems, they can begin their own individual memo workbooks.

3. Likewise, each small group that meets to carry out workplace improvement activities should keep a Big 3 Memo notebook. Problems are no longer written on cards but are written down in the Big 3 Memo. Filling in every space on the memo takes the group through the steps of concretely explaining the problem situation, based on observation. With this understanding of the actual conditions, effective countermeasures can then be implemented.

4. The most suitable divisions are those involved in actual hands-on operations.

5. So far only a few companies have used the Big 3 Memo with production engineering staff. The workbook nevertheless can help these divisions keep a record of trouble spots or problems with equipment that is planned or designed in-house. This information can be used to help prevent recurrences or for educating and training.

6. Product development divisions can use the memo to deal with consumer complaints and concerns about the design and function of the product.

7. Business offices should consider using the memo to attack

office management problems; a number of companies have successfully used this approach. The success in this setting will depend on whether the people involved have the mental flexibility to reorient themselves and see their surroundings in a new light.

Getting Upper Management into the Game

Managers at every level should support and encourage the first-line supervisors in their efforts to use the Big 3 Memo to deal with problems in the workplace. In my managerial roles, I read the memos before I signed off my acknowledgment, and I always signed the memo on the day it was written. It is important for managers to show appreciation to the employees and commend them — and the supervisors who lead the effort — for their insights and hard work.

A good improvement system provides a presentation event as a forum for supervisors to show the results of their teams' efforts to the entire workplace. The supervisor is having a real effect even if he or she does no more than continually ask, "Have you made a Big 3 Memo this week?" Now that I have left Yamaha Motor's manufacturing division, the Big 3 Memo program remains firmly in place for a simple reason: the division manager continually raises the issue with the supervisors.

Introducing the Program: The First Steps

There are differing opinions about whether improvement activities should be mandatory activities or should be pursued on a voluntary basis. Although independent small group activities using the Big 3 Memo are also recommended whenever possible, I think it is important to bring improvement activities directly into the daily line operation. From top management down to the foreman level, it is best to treat the improvement program as "mandatory," in the sense that it is a business imperative.

In my own experiences, when I stated improvement goals and objectives to people at the foremen level in terms of business commands, the requests were carried out quite thoroughly.

When the message was not perceived as a strict business command, it was not given priority. Management has to make improvement one of its own priorities before it can become important to the workers.

At the shop-floor level, the improvement program should be useful to the business operation, but it must also create an atmosphere that accepts individual differences and nurtures development of knowledge and skills. Employees who write improvement proposals take a lot of pride in their ideas and creative effort. Although supervisors need to look at the Big 3 Memos written by their subordinates, it is not appropriate for a supervisor just read someone's memo book. A polite request to look at it is the acceptable approach. The supervisor must show respect for the writer's privacy and individuality.

Sensitive supervisors and managers actually can learn quite a lot from reading people's memos. In reading more Big 3 Memos than probably anyone else, I have discovered that a memo workbook is an expression of the personality of the person who made the entries. As you read memos, you may discover that a person is particularly detail-oriented or has excellent problem detection skills. And you will find out who has a lot of improvement ideas and who can express the essence of a problem in just a few words. You can also realize people's latent talents for expressing the basic elements of the situation by using simple diagrams or illustrations.

Likewise, supervisors who read their subordinates' memos can also gain a better understanding of people's weak points. Rather than seeing them as negative traits, the supervisor can provide personal direction and assistance. The supervisor's helpful feedback and motivation should promote a comfortable working relationship.

Reporting and Recognition

To keep the problem-free engineering program alive throughout the company, it is important to calculate the participation and cost savings every month. Official announcements and displays highlight the company's achievement and monitor the tendency toward lapsing back into the comfortable status quo.

Once a year the factory units and the company as a whole should add up their figures and announce their results publicly. This announcement can be celebrated with a dinner or other event to recognize employees who have made an extra effort to improve their jobs, the workplace, and the company as a whole. Communication and acknowledgment will help maintain pride and interest in the program and contribute continuously to the creating the problem-free workplace.

Postscript

My enthusiasm for eliminating the three basic problems of irrationality, inconsistency, and waste in the workplace has never flagged over the years. I cannot pretend that my methods are the only ones for promoting worksite improvements, but if others find this book even the slightest bit helpful and applicable, my efforts will have been worthwhile.

Finally, I would like to close with these words of the seventeenth-century philosopher Banzan Kumazawa:

"Failure means only that one did not have the motivation. With hard and continuous effort, one will definitely be able to succeed."

Appendix

Figure A-1. Using the Big 3 Memo with the 5S Diagnostic Check Table

5S Diagnostic Check Table	Section:		Worksite:	Group:		Process:		
	Date of check:		Step no.:		Diagnosed by:			
Title	Item	Evaluation Factors				Evaluation	Coefficient	Grade*
Putting in order	Trash, refuse	Is everything in its proper place?						
	Jigs and tools	Are they stored properly and kept ready for use?						
	Equipment	Are there unnecessary things or personal effects?						
	Near equipment	Are there unnecessary things or personal effects?						
Proper arrangement	Aisles between storage areas	Are they clearly marked with lines on the floor?					3	
	Stacking methods	Are things stacked with heavier things lower?						
	"	Are things stacked too high? Have some piles collapsed?						
	Placing methods	Are longer things placed horizontally?						
	"	Is there anything blocking fire extinguishing equipment?						
	Proper arrangement	Are sorting and support partitions installed in the storage area?						
	Proper arrangement	Is anything placed in the aisles?						
	"	Are things placed in a disorderly manner?						
	Bulletin boards	Are they placed so they are easy to see?					3	
	"	Are there dirty or old papers and signs still up?						
	Floors	Are they uneven, damaged, or bumpy?					2	
	"	Are there rubber skids for slippery areas?						
	Idle equipment	Are they labeled with last user and date of last use?						
Cleaning	Floor	Any water or oil stains?					2	
	Any water or oil stains?	Any trash or litter lying around?						
	Chips, scraps	Are there any scattered around?						
	Equipment	Is every part being thoroughly cleaned?						
	Cleaning tools	Do we have everything we need on hand?					2	
Purity	Uniforms	Are they soiled?					2	
	Uniforms	Are they unsafe?						
	Smoking	Is it confined to designated times and areas?						
	Oil	Any leaking or bad smells?						
Adherence	Safety regulations	Are they observed?						
	Personal protective equipment	Are prescribed materials used correctly?					2	
	Caps and helmets	Are they worn properly?						
	Protective clothing	Is it worn properly?						
	Shoes	Are regulation shoes worn?						
	Special items					Evaluation points	(Perfect score = 200 points)	

5-point evaluation system

5 points = Very good!   3 points = Needs a little more effort   1 point = Completely intolerable
4 points = Rather good   2 points = Needs a lot more attention

Standard levels for each step of the   Step 1: 120 points or more   Step 3: 160 points or more
TPM program   Step 2: 140 points or more   Step 4: 180 points or more

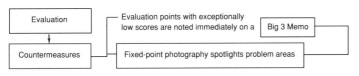

* This Check Table is commonly used to evaluate progress in a TPM program, which is deployed in 4 stages or steps. The grade is determined by multiplying the points earned for each factor by the coefficient assigned to it. Unless another number appears in that column, the coefficient is one. -- Ed.

Figure A-2. The Big 3 Memo and Observing with the Five Senses

Five minutes' careful observation and the Big 3 Memo

(Observing does not mean staring --
rather, it means using all five senses for careful observation)

Whenever you discover a problem point, write it down immediately on a Big 3 Memo

Table of Daily Inspection Points

Item \ Area	Rotating parts	Sliding parts	Driving parts	Transport	Jigs	Holding tanks	Hydraulic equipment	Pneumatic equipment	Lubricating equipment
Oil quantity							👁 (eye)	👁 (eye)	👁 (eye)
Temperature	 ✋ (hand)								
Abnormal sounds	👂 (ear)						👂 (ear)		
Abnormal smell			👃 (nose)						
Vibration	 ✋ (hand)			👁 (eye)		 ✋ (hand)			
Looseness					 ✋ (hand)		 ✋ (hand)		
Damage		👁 (eye)							
Inadequate oil film	👁 (eye)	👁 (eye)							👁 (eye)
Stains			👁 (eye)		👁 (eye)	👁 (eye)			
Leaks							👁 (eye)	👂 (ear)	

Figure A-3. Machine Tool Daily Observation and Maintenance

Time	Subject	Point	Inspection method	Treatment
Before work	Safety equipment	Not functioning	👁	Report to supervisor
	Sliding part	Scratches Oil film	👁	Report to supervisor Check supply quality
	Jigs	Looseness Stains	✋ 👁	Tightening Cleaning
	Hydraulic equipment	Oil quantity Oil film	👁	Check supply level and quality
During operation	Rotating part	Oil film Abnormal sound	👁 👂	Check supply quality Report to supervisor
	Driver	Abnormal smell	👃	Report to supervisor
	Transporting part	Vibration	👁	Report to supervisor
After work	Holding tanks	Stains Vibration	👁 ✋	Cleaning Report to supervisor
	Hydraulic equipment	Leaks Oil quantity	👂 👁	Report to supervisor Supply
	Lubricating equipment	Oil quantity	👁	Supply

Figure A-4. The Big 3 Memo, 5S Activities, and Problem-free Engineering

Problem-free engineering \ 5S	Proper arrangement	Good order	Cleanliness	Cleanup	Adherence

Labor and management cooperating for action

Eliminating small defects and the three basic problems through problem-free engineering

Building a strong workplace in an enterprise determined to win

Air-free

Conveyor-free

Walk-free

Search-free

Inventory-free

Bottleneck-free

Look-free

Wasted motion-free

Air cut-free

Air grind-free

Air press-free

Air stroke-free

Hunger-free

Stack-free

Failure-free

Error-free

Nonstandard-free

Oil pan-free

Machine stock-free

Bolt-free

Dust-free

Accident-free

Corner-free

Rationalizing the flow
- Reducing work-in-process
- Reducing interest rates
- Eliminating wasted space
- Eliminating wasted costs for unnecessary space and transportation
- Strictly meeting delivery dates

Rationalizing operation
- Reducing cycle time
- Raising operating efficiency
- Reducing changeover time
- Reducing labor costs
- Reducing amount of work
- Using less energy
- Creating a safe workplace with good morale

Improving quality
- Eliminating chronic defects
- Eliminating rust, stains, and deterioration
- Making a first-in, first-out system
- Improving quality lifespan
- Gaining confidence of customers

Maintaining safe equipment
- Eliminating chronic breakdowns
- Improving equipment operating rate
- Maintaining precision
- Lengthening lifespan of consumable goods
- Respecting environmental regulations

Carry out immediately   IE and QC activities

Record problems and try hard to solve them

Common terms \ Tool	**Big 3 Memo**

Figure A-5. Basic Industrial Engineering Methods and Major Improvement Objectives

1. Operation Analysis . . . . Improving operation rate (work sampling method)
2. Operator/process analysis . . . . Reducing waiting and moving
3. Product/process analysis . . . . Reducing pile-ups and transport
4. Time research. . . . . Cutting down wasteful operations and time inconsistencies
5. Motion study . . . . Reducing wasteful and awkward movement (qualitatively)
6. PTS method . . . . Reducing wasteful and irrational movements (quantitatively)
   (MTM, Work-Factor, and other methods)
7. Group operation analysis . . . . Reducing waiting
8. Operator/machine analysis . . . . Reducing waiting

Select the best methods to give an accurate analysis of the problem.

Figure A-6. Relationship of Analysis Methods to Process-operation Contents

Classification units	Process	Operation units	Operation factors	Movement factors
Contents	⇨ Carry to lathe ▽ Process delay ○ Machining process ▽ Lot delay ⇨ Carry to inspection □ Inspection	─ Installing tool ─ Checking lubrication ─ Rough machining ─ Finish machining - - - - - - - - - ─ Removing tool ─ Grinding tool	Taking materials ─ Affixing materials ─ Cutting Removing materials	─Reach toward handle Grasp handle ─Rotate handle
Time measurement method	General information	Stopwatch or ordinary watch	Stopwatch	Films, videotapes, PTS tables
Analysis methods	Process analysis	Operation analysis		Motion study

Figure A-7. Therblig Symbols

Type	Operation	Symbol	Explanation of symbol	Example (using a combination screwdriver)
1	Transport empty	⌣	Empty dish	Reaching hand toward screwdriver
	Grasp	∩	Shape of hand grasping	Grasping screwdriver
	Transport loaded	⌣o	Dish carrying something	Bringing screwdriver to the workbench
	Position	9	Object in unstable situation	Screwdriver placed on bench after use
	Assemble	⫲	Fabric, or rectangle put together	Tip of screwdriver installed
	Use	∪	"U"	Screws are tightened
	Disassemble	⫲	Assembled element removed	Removing tip of screwdriver
	Release load	⌢o	Dish with something in it, turned over	Screwdriver released from hand
	Inspect	〇	Lens shape	Checking functioning of screwdriver tip
2	Search	⊂⊃	Side view of searching eye	Searching for the screwdriver
	Find	⊙	Front view of eye	Finding a screwdriver
	Select	→	Arrow indicating choice	Choosing the right size screwdriver
	Plan	ʓ	Person holding head in hand	Deciding screwdriver size according to size of screws
	Pre-position	⛳	Bowling pin	Making adjustments so screwdriver is easier to use
3	Hold	⌂	Magnet attached to steel plate	Holding materials in one hand
	Rest for overcoming fatigue	⎰	Person sitting down	Taking a break from the operation
	Unavoidable delay	⌒o	Person who has fallen down	Process and lot delay
	Avoidable delay	⌣o	Person sleeping	Shooting the breeze instead of working

Note: Therbligs represent the basic elemental motions identified by two of the pioneers of motion study, Frank and Lillian Gilbreth (the word itself is an anagram of their last name). These symbols or abbreviations were used in conjunction with frame-by-frame analysis of a filmed operation to study the effectiveness of various work motions. The American Society of Mechanical Engineers uses a set of similar work elements for motion study. -- Ed.

Figure A-8. The Seven QC Tools

1. Cause-and-effect (fishbone or Ishikawa) diagram . . . . Shows causal relationships
2. Pareto curve . . . . Points out serious defects or problems
3. Histogram . . . . Displays problem distribution
4. Check sheet . . . . Collects problem distribution data
5. Control chart . . . . Shows variation from standard values
6. Stratification . . . . Compares measured differences between groups
7. Scatter diagram . . . . Charts correlations between two sets of data

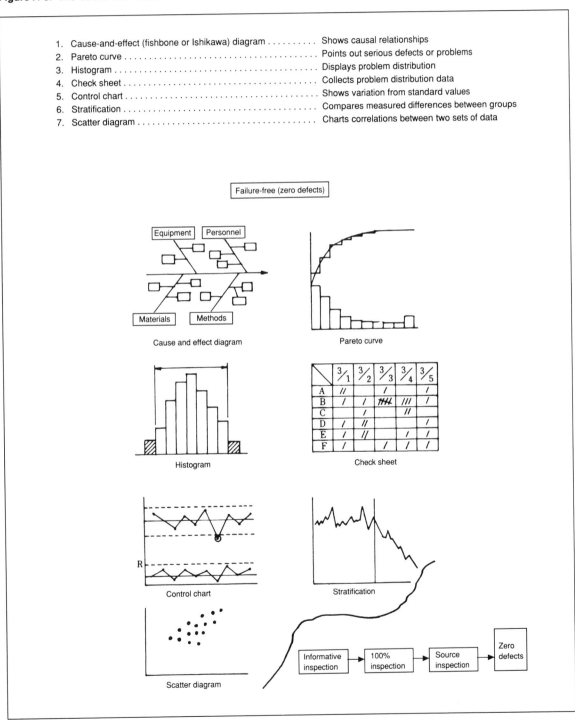

Failure-free (zero defects)

Cause and effect diagram

Pareto curve

Histogram

Check sheet

Control chart

Stratification

Scatter diagram

Informative inspection → 100% inspection → Source inspection → Zero defects

Figure A-9. Cost Reduction Reference Sheet Example (Factory F)

Problem-free engineering	Type of efficiency	Cost savings		Standard values		

Row 1

Problem-free engineering	Type of efficiency
Walk-free Look-free Search-free Wasted motion-free Air cut-free Air press-free Short stop-free Bottleneck-free Call-free Meeting-free	Reducing time

Labor costs (yen)

1 sec.	0.60
1 min.	36
1 hr.	2,160
1 day	16,380
1 month	360,000

(Walk-free)

Number of steps	Distance	Time	Cost (yen)
1 step	0.75 m	1.6 sec.	0.96
2 steps	1.5 m	3.2 sec.	1.92
10 steps	7.5 m	16 sec.	9.60
100 steps	75 m	160 sec.	96

Press depreciation (yen)

500 ton	66/min.
300-350	43/min.
0-250	15/min.

Let's work together to break the time barrier!

Quality = Number of defects reduced x Selling price

Row 2

Problem-free engineering	Type of efficiency
Air-free Conveyor-free Oil pan-free Stack-free Inventory-free	Use of equipment

Floor surface area 1 m² = ¥1,000/month

Space 1 m³ = ¥3,000/month

It's great to free all this space!

Row 3

Problem-free engineering	Type of efficiency
Bolt-free Part-free Welding-free	Parts and materials needed

Nuts: 1 unit = ¥1
Bolts: 1 unit = ¥1
Paper: 1 sheet = ¥1
Copying: 1 page = ¥10
Spot welding: 1 spot = ¥3
Welding: 1 cm = ¥4

PP band 1 m = ¥2
Packing tape 2" x 1 m = ¥2
3/4" x 1 m = ¥3
Strapping tape 2" x 1 m = ¥3
3/4" x 1 m = ¥5
Cellophane tape 1 m = ¥2.50

Cost savings from improvements ...Compute the total efficiency resulting from various "_____-free" items

Computing for seasonal production (using half-year figures)..When production is done for only 2 months, for example,
savings for 1 month is ¥4500, calculate the annual savings as:
and the cost ¥4500/month x 2/6 months = ¥1500.

For values not listed here, ask your supervisor.

Figure A-10. Cost Reduction Reference Sheet Example (Company Y)

Monthly Cost Savings and Efficiency Points Resulting from Improvements

A. Cost reductions from efficiency improvements

1. Reducing operating time	Cost reduction = ¥30/min. x min. reduced/month
2. Reducing labor costs for an operation	" = ¥300,000/month x number of workers
3. Reducing materials costs	" = number reduced/month x unit cost
4. Reducing space	" = ¥1,000/month x m^2 saved
5. Reduced new equipment needs (spread over 3 years)	" = Price x 1/3 x 1/12
6. Reducing inventory expenses by shortening lead time	" = Inventory expenses saved/month x 0.01 including process evaluation (when impossible, minutes per process, etc.)
7. Efficiency for other matters	" = Amount saved/month

B. Efficiency points (for improvement "point system")

Paperwork reduction	(efficiency points) = (surface area reduction) m^2/month ÷ 246
Weight reduction	(") = (weight reduction) kg/month ÷ 14

C. Standard costs for calculation

1. Unit costs

LPG	¥73/kg
Fuel oil	¥78/liter
Electricity	¥20/kilowatt (¥.02/Watt)
Drinking water	¥240/metric ton
Industrial water	¥140/metric ton
Air	¥210/hr. from a Ø10 mm hole

Figure A-10. Cost Reduction Reference Sheet Example (Company Y) (continued)

2a. Applied examples

Item	Contents	Cost
LPG	Burning propane gas for 1 day: .2 m3/hr. x 2.5 kg3/m x ¥73/kg x 24 hr.	¥876/day
Fuel oil	Operating boiler for 1 day: 700 liters x ¥78/liter	¥54,600/day
Electricity	Burning fluorescent lights for 1 day 2 lamps x 40 W/hr. x ¥0.02/W x 24 hr.	¥39/day
Drinking water	Running water continuously for 1 day 1.14 kiloliter/hr. x ¥240/kiloliter x 24 hr.	¥6,566/day

2b. Example: Cost of air leak neglected for 1 day

Diameter of leaking hole	Cost from losses (yen/day)	Diameter of leaking hole	Cost from losses (yen/day)
1 mm	77	8 mm	3975
2 mm	260	9 mm	5033
3 mm	562	10 mm	6178
4 mm	994	11 mm	7517
5 mm	1556	12 mm	8920
6 mm	2246	13 mm	10476
7 mm	3070	14 mm	12096

Additional References

1. *Methods of Generating Worksite Improvement Ideas at Yamaha Motor*, Tomō Sugiyama (Nikkan Shobo)
2. *How to Cultivate Improvement Ideas*, Tomō Sugiyama (Nikkan Shobo)
3. *Improvement Stories*, Tomō Sugiyama (Japan Management Association)
4. *Factory Management* magazine, December 1984 (Nikkan Kogyo Shimbunsha)
   - "How to Encourage Improvement Ideas and Double the Number of Suggestions," Tomō Sugiyama
   - "Improving the Workplace with ' -free Engineering' and the Big 3 Memo," Kazuho Yoshimoto and Norio Suzuki
5. *5S Techniques*, multiple authors (Nikkan Kogyo Shimbunsha)
6. *Easy TPM*, Yamaha Motor Corp., Ltd. (Technical Skills Association
7. *Promoting Easy IE*, Norio Suzuki (Japan Management Association)
8. *Factory Management* magazine, August 1987 (Nikkan Kogyo Shimbunsha) "Eliminating Waste through the Idea of Problem-free Engineering and the Big 3 Memo," Tomō Sugiyama
9. *The Toyota Production System*, Toyota Motor Corp. (on cost cutting)

About the Author

Tomō Sugiyama is a full-time instructor with the Japan Management Association (JMA) Management School and a consultant in factory management. He began his career with Nippon Gakki Company in 1935 and after World War II was put in charge of machining techniques for materials in the Woodworking Division. In 1952 he became Efficiency Section Chief and participated in planning and promoting a conveyor system for piano production. When Yamaha Motors, a subsidiary of Nippon Gakki, became a separate company in 1955, Mr. Sugiyama joined as Production Section Chief. In 1959 he returned to Nippon Gakki and in 1960 became managing director of the Showa factory.

In 1963 Mr. Sugiyama was named a representative director of Kitagawa Automobile Industries, Ltd. (an affiliate of Yamaha Motor now known as Yamaha Automotive Industries). He was appointed to the board of directors of Yamaha Motors in 1966 and in 1980 was given the concurrent position of president of Yamaha Engineering, Ltd. From 1982 to the present he has been retired.

Mr. Sugiyama was one of 356 people decorated by the prime minister as members of the All Japan Industrial Technology Corps in 1941. Contributions for which he was awarded include devising a bamboo substitute for the springs used in organ airboxes during World War II, when steel could not be used. In 1980, he received the Japan IE Association literary award for his treatise on "Women-oriented Labor Management." His major works include *Methods of Generating Worksite Improvement Ideas at Yamaha Motors* and *How to Cultivate Improvement Ideas*. At the 1986 Japan IE Conference, Mr. Sugiyama was awarded a letter of appreciation for meritorious service.

Index

Other Books on Continuous Improvement

Productivity Press publishes and distributes materials on continuous improvement in productivity, quality, customer service, and the creative involvement of all employees. Many of our products are direct source materials from Japan that have been translated into English for the first time and are available exclusively from Productivity. Supplemental products and services include newsletters, conferences, seminars, in-house training and consulting, audio-visual training programs, and industrial study missions. Send for our free book catalog.

Managerial Engineering
Techniques for Improving Quality and Productivity in the Workplace

by Ryuji Fukuda

A proven path to managerial success, based on reliable methods developed by one of Japan's leading productivity experts and winner of the coveted Deming Prize for quality. Dr. W. Edwards Deming, world-famous consultant on quality, says that the book "provides an excellent and clear description of the devotion and methods of Japanese management to continual improvement of quality." (CEDAC training programs also available.)
ISBN 0-915299-09-7 / 206 pages / $34.95 / ME-BK

Poka-Yoke
Improving Product Quality by Preventing Defects

compiled by Nikkan Kogyo Shimbun, Ltd./Factory Magazine (ed.)
preface by Shigeo Shingo

If your goal is 100% zero defects, here is the book for you — a completely illustrated guide to poka-yoke (mistake-proofing) for supervisors and shop-floor workers. Many poka-yoke devices come from line workers and are implemented with the help of engineering staff. The result is better product quality — and greater participation by workers in efforts to improve your processes, your products, and your company as a whole.
ISBN 0-915299-31-3 / 288 pages / $59.95 / Order code IPOKA-BK

Productivity Press, Inc., Dept. BK, P.O. Box 3007, Cambridge, MA 02140 1-800-274-9911

A Study of the Toyota Production System
From an Industrial Engineering Viewpoint (rev.)

by Shigeo Shingo

The "green book" that started it all — the first book in English on JIT, now completely revised and re-translated. Here is Dr. Shingo's classic industrial engineering rationale for the priority of process-based over operational improvements for manufacturing. He explains the basic mechanisms of the Toyota production system in a practical and simple way so that you can apply them in your own plant.
ISBN 0-915299-17-8 / 352 pages / Price $39.95 / Order code STREV-BK

TPM Development Program
Implementing Total Productive Maintenance

edited by Seiichi Nakajima

This book outlines a three-year program for systematic TPM development and implementation. It describes in detail the five principal developmental activities of TPM:
1. Systematic elimination of the six big equipment related losses through small group activities
2. Autonomous maintenance (by operators)
3. Scheduled maintenance for the maintenance department
4. Training in operation and maintenance skills
5. Comprehensive equipment management from the design stage
ISBN 0-915299-37-2 / 528 pages / $85.00 / Order code DTPM-BK

JIT Factory Revolution
A Pictorial Guide to Factory Design of the Future

Hiroyuki Hirano/JIT Management Library

Here at last is the first-ever encyclopedic picture book of JIT. Using 240 pages of photos, cartoons, and diagrams, this unprecedented behind-the-scenes look at actual production and assembly plants shows you exactly how JIT looks and functions. It shows you how to set up each area of a JIT plant and provides hundreds of useful ideas you can implement. If you've made the crucial decision to run production using JIT and want to show your employees what it's all about, this book is a must. The photographs, from various Japanese production and assembly plants, provide vivid depictions of what work is like in a JIT environment. And the text, simple and easy to read, makes all the essentials crystal clear.
ISBN 0-915299-44-5 / 218 pages / illustrated / $49.95 / Order code JITFAC-BK

Productivity Press, Inc., Dept. BK, P.O. Box 3007, Cambridge, MA 02140 1-800-274-9911

The Idea Book
Improvement Through Total Employee Involvement
edited by the Japan Human Relations Association

What would your company be like if each employee — from line workers to engineers to sales people — gave 100 ideas every year for improving the company? This handbook of Japanese-style suggestion systems (called "teian"), will help your company develop its own vital improvement system by getting all employees involved. Train workers how to write improvement proposals, help supervisors promote participation, and put creative problem solving to work in your company. Designed as a self-trainer and study group tool, the book is heavily illustrated and includes hundreds of examples.
ISBN 0-915299-22-4 / 232 pages / $49.95 / Order code IDEA-BK

Productivity Press, Inc., Dept. BK, P.O. Box 3007, Cambridge, MA 02140 1-800-274-9911

BOOKS AVAILABLE FROM PRODUCTIVITY PRESS

Nikkan Kogyo Shimbun, Ltd./ Factory Magazine (ed.). **Poka-yoke: Improving Product Quality by Preventing Defects**
ISBN 0-915299-31-3 / 1989 / 288 pages / $59.95 / order code IPOKA

Ohno, Taiichi. **Toyota Production System: Beyond Large-Scale Production**
ISBN 0-915299-14-3 / 1988 / 163 pages / $39.95 / order code OTPS

Ohno, Taiichi. **Workplace Management**
ISBN 0-915299-19-4 / 1988 / 165 pages / $34.95 / order code WPM

Ohno, Taiichi and Setsuo Mito. **Just-In-Time for Today and Tomorrow**
ISBN 0-915299-20-8 / 1988 / 208 pages / $34.95 / order code OMJIT

Psarouthakis, John. **Better Makes Us Best**
ISBN 0-915299-56-9 / 1989 / 112 pages / $16.95 / order code BMUB

Shingo, Shigeo. **Non-Stock Production: The Shingo System for Continuous Improvement**
ISBN 0-915299-30-5 / 1988 / 480 pages / $75.00 / order code NON

Shingo, Shigeo. **A Revolution In Manufacturing: The SMED System**, *Translated by Andrew P. Dillon*
ISBN 0-915299-03-8 / 1985 / 383 pages / $65.00 / order code SMED

Shingo, Shigeo. **The Sayings of Shigeo Shingo: Key Strategies for Plant Improvement**, *Translated by Andrew P. Dillon*
ISBN 0-915299-15-1 / 1987 / 208 pages / $36.95 / order code SAY

Shingo, Shigeo. **A Study of the Toyota Production System from an Industrial Engineering Viewpoint** (Revised Ed.)
ISBN 0-915299-17-8 / 1989 / 352 pages / $39.95 / order code STREV

Shingo, Shigeo. **Zero Quality Control: Source Inspection and the Poka-yoke System**, *Translated by Andrew P. Dillon*
ISBN 0-915299-07-0 / 1986 / 328 pages / $65.00 / order code ZQC

Shinohara, Isao (ed.). **New Production System: JIT Crossing Industry Boundaries**
ISBN 0-915299-21-6 / 1988 / 224 pages / $34.95 / order code NPS

Sugiyama, Tomō. **The Improvement Book: Creating the Problem-free Workplace**
ISBN 0-915299-47-X / 1989 / 320 pages / $49.95 / order code IB

Tateisi, Kazuma. **The Eternal Venture Spirit: An Executive's Practical Philosophy**
ISBN 0-915299-55-0 / 1989 / 208 pages / $19.95 / order code EVS

Productivity Press, Inc., Dept. BK, P.O. Box 3007, Cambridge, MA 02140 1-800-274-9911

AUDIO-VISUAL PROGRAMS

Japan Management Association. **Total Productive Maintenance: Maximizing Productivity and Quality**
ISBN 0-915299-46-1 / 167 slides / 1989 / $749.00 / order code STPM
ISBN 0-915299-49-6 / 2 videos / 1989 / $749.00 / order code VTPM

Shingo, Shigeo. **The SMED System**, *Translated by Andrew P. Dillon*
ISBN 0-915299-11-9 / 181 slides / 1986 / $749.00 / order code S5
ISBN 0-915299-27-5 / 2 videos / 1987 / $749.00 / order code V5

Shingo, Shigeo. **The Poka-yoke System**, *Translated by Andrew P. Dillon*
ISBN 0-915299-13-5 / 235 slides / 1987 / $749.00 / order code S6
ISBN 0-915299-28-3 / 2 videos / 1987 / $749.00 / order code V6

TO ORDER: Write, phone, or fax Productivity Press, Dept. BK, P.O. Box 3007, Cambridge, MA 02140, phone 1-800-274-9911, fax 617-868-3524. Send check or charge to your credit card (American Express, Visa, MasterCard accepted).

U.S. ORDERS: Add $4 shipping for first book, $2 each additional. CT residents add
7.5% and MA residents 5% sales tax.

FOREIGN ORDERS: Payment must be made in U.S. dollars (checks must be drawn on U.S. banks). For Canadian orders, add $10 shipping for first book, $2 each
additional. For orders to other countries write, phone, or fax for quote and indicate shipping method desired.

NOTE: Prices subject to change without notice.

The Improvement Book

Creating the
Problem-free Workplace

The Big 3 Memo Workbook

Productivity Press
P.O. Box 3007
Cambridge, MA 02140
(617) 497-5146

Translated by Bruce Talbot
Cover design by Donna Puleo
Typeset by Rudra Press, Cambridge, MA
Printed and bound by the Courier Book Companies
Printed in the United States of America

ISBN 0-915299-72-0

89 90 91 10 9 8 7 6 5 4 3 2 1

Contents

How to Use the Big 3 Memo Workbook

The purpose of this workbook is to help employees and supervisors keep a keen eye on their workplaces and to improve their insight into what goes on there. It is also meant to be used as a daily log for recording improvement-related ideas.

When you notice one of the three basic problems in the workplace, you are not compelled to immediately come up with a complete improvement proposal. Instead, use this workbook freely just to note problems. If an improvement idea comes to mind later on, then you can add a description of your proposal, keeping track of the stages of its development. The workbook thus becomes a resource of facts and research to refer to during the implementation of your proposal or during other improvement-related activities at your company.

Please make full use of the front sections of the workbook, which include a lot of valuable information. For full instructions about using the memo and log sheet, see Chapter 4 of *The Improvement Book*. The most important thing is to take a cold, hard five-minute look at your workplace at least once a day.

Four Ways to Improve the Workplace

1. Take a Cold, Hard Five-minute Look at Each Process

- Use the 5W1H approach: Ask "Why? What? Where? When? Who? and How?"
- Go beyond the first "Why?": Ask "Why?" at least five times to discover the root cause.

2. Whenever, Wherever — Make a Big 3 Memo

- Whenever or wherever you notice any of the three basic problems (irrationality, inconsistency, and waste), immediately record the problem for future improvement.

3. Use the 5S Industrial Housekeeping Techniques

(1) *Putting in Order:* Sort items and discard useless things.
(2) *Proper Arrangement:* Arrange things so you can easily get to what you need.

(3) *Cleaning:* Make the workplace spotless and check for maintenance problems.

(4) *Purity:* Maintain cleanliness throughout the workday.

(5) *Adherence:* Commitment to good habits leads to good work.

4. Popularize the "Problem-free" Concepts

- *-free Engineering* = a method of eliminating waste. Use these terms to spread awareness of problems that can be improved.

- *Fixed-point Photography:* A way to reflect problem points and short-comings. Use the same camera in the same position to continuously expose situations that might otherwise go unnoticed.

- *Single-point Management:* Handle key problem points during the planning stage. Spend more energy on planning and less on trouble-shooting.

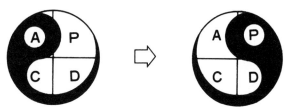

- *"Wanted":* Track down the culprits during the trial operation stage. Make good use of design specification check sheets.

Big 3 Memo Log Sheet

(Name)

File No.	Subject	Observation points			Date observed			Month			Savings/ month	Cumulative savings	Comments	Grade
		Irrationality	Inconsistency	Waste	MTH	DAY	YR	MTH	DAY	YR				

Cumulative monthly cost savings	Mth/Day/Yr						
	Amount saved						

Big 3 Memo Log Sheet

(Name)

File No.	Subject	Observation points			Date observed			Month			Savings/ month	Cumulative savings	Comments	Grade
		Irrationality	Inconsistency	Waste	MTH	DAY	YR	MTH	DAY	YR				

Cumulative monthly cost savings	Mth/Day/Yr						
	Amount saved						

Hints for Using the Big 3 Memo

Defining the Big Three Problems

	Meaning
Irrationality	1. Things that are hard to reach or difficult to do 2. Things that don't make sense or are hard to find reasons for 3. Things you do just because you are told to do them
Inconsistency	1. Uneven color, texture, or material thickness 2. General irregularity or nonuniformity
Waste	1. Things that do not help anything 2. Things that are not profitable

Irrational actions

Get rid of actions or operations that cause undue fatigue. Causes of fatigue include:

1. Work that takes a lot of physical effort
2. Work that makes you stoop over
3. Work that requires long periods of vigilance, including:
   - Having to remember lots of things
   - Constantly worrying about defects or breakdowns
   - Struggling to read illegible words or symbols

LET'S GET RID OF ALL THIS!

Inconsistent actions

Sometimes our enthusiasm for our work gets us carried away to the point that we add a "personal touch" that can easily result in inconsistent quality. Such inconsistency can also give rise to irrationality and waste, so it is important to adhere to standards.

Wasteful actions

Get rid of operations and work procedures that do not add to profitability. Such unprofitable actions include:

1. Work procedures that make you stack or rearrange materials, parts, products, or tools
2. Work that makes you take one or more steps
3. Work that makes you wait (such as waiting for other operations or machines)
4. Operations or work procedures that are created by problems, such as looking for misplaced items, cleaning up messes, repairs, tune-ups, and inspections
5. Operations that slow down your working pace, such as waiting for materials or parts to be delivered, turning something around, and unnecessary sorting

LET'S GET RID OF AS MANY OF THESE AS WE CAN!

Applying the Principles of Motion Economy

The principles of motion economy help reduce fatigue and raise productivity.

1. Move both arms in unison or move them symmetrically, but do not move just one arm at a time.

What is the best way to take the cap off this ink bottle?

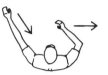

(1) Get the ink bottle

(2) Take off the cap

Before improvement

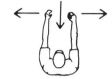

(3) Take off the cap while getting the bottle

After improvement

2. The following illustration shows the correlation between arm movement and working time.

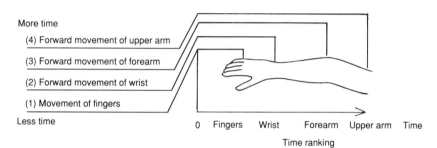

More time

(4) Forward movement of upper arm

(3) Forward movement of forearm

(2) Forward movement of wrist

(1) Movement of fingers

Less time

0   Fingers   Wrist   Forearm   Upper arm   Time

Time ranking

The point is to minimize body movement by limiting movement to body parts with low time rankings while still performing the job satisfactorily. Add up the body motions in terms of their rank numbers (1 through 4) and discover how to do the work with as low a total as possible. The less movement you perform, the less energy you expend and the less tired you become.

3. You can minimize fatigue by repeating motions with a natural feeling of rhythm and by making your curved movements as smooth as possible. Do as little holding or adjusting of materials as you can. Use stands or jigs to hold your materials and/or tools for you. Try to keep both hands involved in your work.

4. Keep materials and tools in specified places in front of and around you. Lay them out to be picked up in the order that you routinely use them.

Figure 1 Layout of Work Area

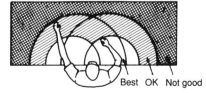

Best OK Not good

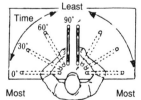

Least

Time   90°
    60°
30°
0°   Most

Most

Figure 2 Example

As shown in Figure 2, if you are inserting the end of a pin held at an angle of zero degrees from the workbench, you cannot avoid twisting your head to see where you are inserting it. The closer you get to inserting it at a 90-degree angle (directlyin front of you), the less time and effort you will waste in turning your head. Therefore, the 90-degree angle is the work position for minimizing time and effort.

9

5. Try to keep from fighting gravity with the materials you are handling; wherever possible, move them down, not up. See if you can use a chute or other device to transport your product away by its own gravity.

6. Try to set your stool, chair, or desk at the most comfortable position and make sure your lighting is bright enough and at a good angle.

7. If you utilize your legs and feet, you can lighten the load on your arms and hands. However, be sure to avoid having to move your feet around a lot or having to take steps.

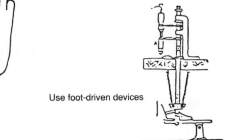

Use foot-driven devices

8. Side-to-side eye movements are less tiring than up-and-down ones. Arrange your work to avoid eye fatigue.

9. Whenever possible, combine procedures, using your tools as extensions of your hands and feet. Try to combine two or more tools into one.

Combination pliers/screwdriver

Pliers

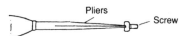

Screw

The Big 3 Memo Matrix

There are many ways to observe irrationality, inconsistency, and waste.

Observation Points \ Problem-free Engineering Examples	A Air-free	B Conveyor-free	C Bolt-free	D Burr-free	E Weight-free	F Bottleneck-free	G Look-free	H Walk-free	I Air cut-free	J Air grind-free	K Air press-free	L Stack-free	M Paper-free	N _____-free
1 People														
2 Skills														
3 Methods														
4 Time														
5 Equipment														
6 Jigs and tools														
7 Materials														
8 Production output														
9 Inventory volume														
10 Location														
11 Way of thinking														
12 Other														

A (Air-free): Don't just move empty air around or reserve places for it. Get rid of any use of space that does not create added value.

B (Conveyor-free): Are conveyors being used as places to leave parts? Are operations really flowing or do they just appear that way?

C (Bolt-free): The number of assembly tasks is proportional to the number of bolts used. Reducing the bolt requirements can also save time in retooling.

D (Burr-free): Promote designs that eliminate burr formation. Incorporate any unavoidable deburring in the process immediately following punching.

E (Weight-free): Can the materials or tools safely be made any lighter? Find ways to manipulate heavy things with a light touch.

F (Bottleneck-free): Are bottlenecks appearing anywhere along the line? Eliminate them as they appear to streamline the process.

G (Look-free): Are people standing idle at any time? People simply watching their machines work are not working.

H (Walk-free): Walking around is not really working, either. Even two or three needless steps can add up to a big waste of time and energy.

I (Air cut-free): Are cutters operating during an excessively long stroke? Until a cutter begins cutting a workpiece, its use is wasting energy.

J (Air grind-free): Are grinders wastefully grinding air? Listen for whether or not they are actually grinding anything.

K (Air press-free): Are press strokes so long that they are wastefully pressing air?

L (Stack-free): Are materials or parts stacking up anywhere? Arrange things differently to get rid of pileups.

M (Paper-free): Do people really need to hold the papers or clipboards they are using? Wherever possible, try to eliminate unnecessary paperwork.

N (_____-free): Many other examples can be found. Try coming up with one of your own.

11

Ten Guidelines for Effective Use of the Big 3 Memo

1. For Managers

To carry out your daily duties successfully, you have to resolve any difficulties or obstacles that come up. Things that happen in the spur of the moment are easily forgotten. Why not make a note of the problem on a Big 3 Memo, to help remind you to work on a solution?

2. For Supervisors

Have a good look at your own workplace and do whatever you can personally to improve it. As soon as you discover a problem, write it down in the Big 3 Memo book, then see what you can do to solve it. If you find that you can't solve it on your own, get other people to join you in solving it. Support the problem-solving efforts of your subordinates.

3. For General Employees

Take a good five-minute look at your own area and work methods, or get someone else to carefully watch you work for five minutes. You'd be surprised how this can point out things to note in a Big 3 Memo. And that can lead to improvement proposals. No one knows more about the work than you do, so your observations and ideas are particularly important in creating a problem-free workplace.

4. Help Catch the Culprits Red-handed

When you have a problem, stop a minute before you launch into the long, involved business of retracing the past, compiling data, and creating statistics. First, take a good look at the processes, things, and workplaces involved and keep an eye out for the cause of the problem. With observation, you can sometimes catch the culprit (cause) red-handed, without extensive factual research.

5. Help Prevent "Crimes"

Even when you don't see any problems during your five-minute observation, you may find things that seem likely to cause problems in the future, and you can often begin taking preventive measures by noting these things down in your Big 3 Memo. Doing this may take more than just five minutes — finding such latent causes takes a lot of insight and thought. But if you do it, you can prevent "crimes" (problems) from occurring.

In quality control, managing things at their source goes a long way toward achieving zero defects, zero breakdowns, and zero short line stops.

6. Use the Big 3 Memo to Keep Track of the Cost Savings from Improvements

The cost-saving effects of improvement activities conducted in the workplace are too easily forgotten and ignored. By noting everything related to the improvement in a Big 3 Memo and entering the numbers on the log sheets, the information will be there when it's time to compile the financial reports.

Many small improvements = one big success!

7. Help Line Operators and Technical Staff Follow a Common Strategy

Problems noted on Big 3 Memos can be classified into those that can be solved right away and those that cannot be. "Unsolvable" problems often include problems whose solutions require drastic measures, such as a complete change in the layout of the workplace. In order to solve these problems, we have to discover the actual limitations of the situation: how far we can go.

Such drastic measures obviously require the participation of engineering staff. Maintenance staff frequently is also involved. Since the line supervisors or small group leaders are responsible for figuring out the precise needs for making each improvement in their workplace, good communication between them and the technical and maintenance staff is essential. It is quite possible for line people and staff people to follow a common strategy and work for a common cause.

8. Keep your Big 3 Memos Well Organized

While it's true that the Big 3 Memo is a study aid, a diary-type daily logbook, and a know-how collection all in one, it is important that these different notebook functions be kept organized and not all jumbled together. Try to use all parts of the workbook, from the handbook sections in front, to the memo forms (top and bottom), to the log sheets (remember to keep track of all of your ideas).

9. Use Big 3 Memos in Small Group Activities

Each circle or team should have its own Big 3 Memo workbook for addressing problems observed in the course of small group activities. Group members can use it to jot down problem descriptions and ideas and to refer to during the activities. During brainstorming for "problem-free engineering" themes, the Big 3 Memo's easy-to-use terminology can help members come up with ideas and solutions.

10. Use the Big 3 Memo as a Springboard for Innovation

Innovative proposals are often motivated by a desire to solve problems such as backbreaking labor, hazardous conditions, wastefulness, or jobs that make workers feel uneasy, limited, or resigned to failure. That is why it is important to jot down such problems in a Big 3 Memo for future use. It is often from a humble beginning, such as a simple Big 3 Memo, that a big innovation is born.

PROBLEM-FREE ENGINEERING BY FACTORY MANAGEMENT AREA

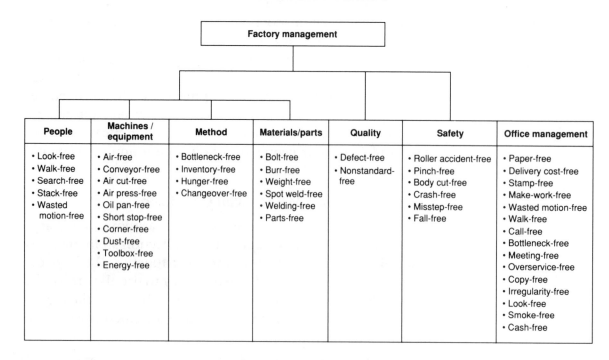

People	Machines / equipment	Method	Materials/parts	Quality	Safety	Office management
• Look-free • Walk-free • Search-free • Stack-free • Wasted motion-free	• Air-free • Conveyor-free • Air cut-free • Air press-free • Oil pan-free • Short stop-free • Corner-free • Dust-free • Toolbox-free • Energy-free	• Bottleneck-free • Inventory-free • Hunger-free • Changeover-free	• Bolt-free • Burr-free • Weight-free • Spot weld-free • Welding-free • Parts-free	• Defect-free • Nonstandard-free	• Roller accident-free • Pinch-free • Body cut-free • Crash-free • Misstep-free • Fall-free	• Paper-free • Delivery cost-free • Stamp-free • Make-work-free • Wasted motion-free • Walk-free • Call-free • Bottleneck-free • Meeting-free • Overservice-free • Copy-free • Irregularity-free • Look-free • Smoke-free • Cash-free

HOW TO PROMOTE IMPROVEMENTS WITH THE BIG 3 MEMO PROGRAM

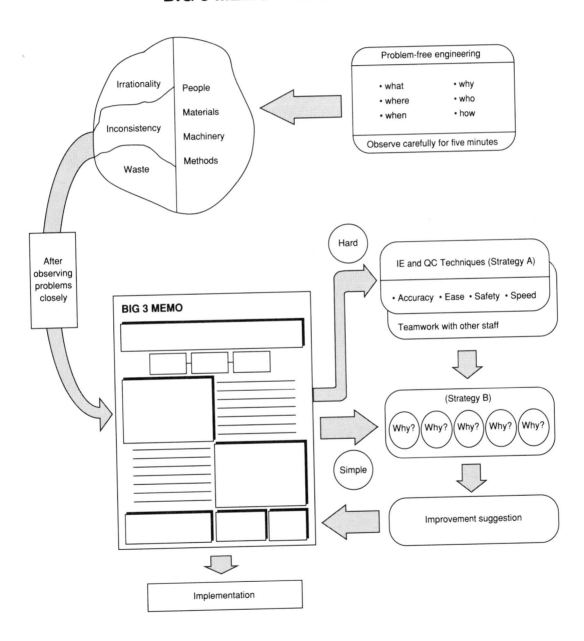

5 minutes of careful observation . . .

BIG 3 MEMO

Write a memo whenever you see a problem

File No.

| Name: | Section: | Worksite: | Group: |

| Machine Type: | Line/Parts: | Process: |

Observation Points:

Point

-free Engineering

-free

Big 3 Problem

Irrationality

Inconsistency

Waste

Use the Big 3 Memo to find observation points.

Present Condition

Date:

Observation: _____

After Improvements: _____

After Improvement

Date:

Improvement Points

Results

Cost Savings/Gain:

Suggestion No.

Grade:

5 minutes of careful observation . . .

BIG 3 MEMO

Write a memo whenever you see a problem

File No.

Name:	Section:	Worksite:	Group:
Machine Type:	Line/Parts:	Process:	

Observation Points:

Point	-free Engineering	Big 3 Problem
	-free	Irrationality
		Inconsistency
		Waste

Use the Big 3 Memo to find observation points.

Present Condition

Date:

Observation: _____

After Improvements: _____

After Improvement

Date:

Improvement Points	Results	Suggestion No.
	Cost Savings/Gain:	Grade:

18

5 minutes of careful observation . . .

BIG 3 MEMO

File No.

Write a memo whenever you see a problem

Name:	Section:	Worksite:	Group:

Machine Type:	Line/Parts:	Process:

Observation Points:

Point	-free Engineering	Big 3 Problem
	-free	Irrationality Inconsistency Waste

Use the Big 3 Memo to find observation points.

Present Condition

Date:

Observation:

After Improvements:

After Improvement

Date:

Improvement Points

Results

Cost Savings/Gain:

Suggestion No.

Grade:

19

5 minutes of careful observation . . .

BIG 3 MEMO

Write a memo whenever you see a problem

File No.

Name:	Section:	Worksite:	Group:
Machine Type:	Line/Parts:	Process:	

Observation Points:

Point

-free Engineering

-free

Big 3 Problem

Irrationality

Inconsistency

Waste

Use the Big 3 Memo to find observation points.

Present Condition

Date:

Observation:

After Improvements:

After Improvement

Date:

Improvement Points

Results

Cost Savings/Gain:

Suggestion No.

Grade:

5 minutes of careful observation . . .

BIG 3 MEMO

Write a memo whenever you see a problem

File No.

Name:	Section:	Worksite:	Group:

Machine Type:	Line/Parts:	Process:

Observation Points:

Point

-free Engineering

-free

Big 3 Problem

Irrationality

Inconsistency

Waste

Use the Big 3 Memo to find observation points.

Present Condition

Date:

Observation: _____

_____

_____

_____

_____

_____

_____

_____

After Improvements: _____

_____

_____

_____

_____

_____

_____

After Improvement

Date:

Improvement Points

Results

Cost Savings/Gain:

Suggestion No.

Grade:

21

5 minutes of careful observation . . .

BIG 3 MEMO

Write a memo whenever you see a problem

| Name: | Section: | Worksite: | Group: |

| Machine Type: | Line/Parts: | Process: |

Observation Points:

Point

-free Engineering

-free

Big 3 Problem

Irrationality

Inconsistency

Waste

Use the Big 3 Memo to find observation points.

Present Condition

Date:

Observation: _____

_____

_____

_____

_____

_____

_____

After Improvements: _____

_____

_____

_____

_____

_____

After Improvement

Date:

Improvement Points

Results

Suggestion No.

Cost Savings/Gain:

Grade:

5 minutes of careful observation . . .

BIG 3 MEMO

File No.

Write a memo whenever you see a problem

| Name: | Section: | Worksite: | Group: |

| Machine Type: | Line/Parts: | Process: |

Observation Points:

Point	-free Engineering	Big 3 Problem
	-free	Irrationality
		Inconsistency
		Waste

Use the Big 3 Memo to find observation points.

Present Condition

Date:

Observation: _____

After Improvements: _____

After Improvement

Date:

Improvement Points

Results

Cost Savings/Gain:

Suggestion No.

Grade:

23

5 minutes of careful observation . . .

BIG 3 MEMO

Write a memo whenever you see a problem

File No.

Name:	Section:	Worksite:	Group:

Machine Type:	Line/Parts:	Process:

Observation Points:

Point

-free Engineering
-free

Big 3 Problem
Irrationality
Inconsistency
Waste

Use the Big 3 Memo to find observation points.

Present Condition

Date:

Observation:

After Improvements:

After Improvement

Date:

Improvement Points

Results

Cost Savings/Gain:

Suggestion No.

Grade:

5 minutes of careful observation . . .

BIG 3 MEMO

Write a memo whenever you see a problem

File No.

Name:	Section:	Worksite:	Group:

Machine Type:	Line/Parts:	Process:

Observation Points:

Point

-free Engineering

-free

Big 3 Problem

Irrationality

Inconsistency

Waste

Use the Big 3 Memo to find observation points.

Present Condition

Date:

Observation: _____

After Improvements: _____

After Improvement

Date:

Improvement Points

Results

Cost Savings/Gain:

Suggestion No.

Grade:

5 minutes of careful observation . . .

BIG 3 MEMO

File No.

Write a memo whenever you see a problem

| Name: | Section: | Worksite: | Group: |
| Machine Type: | Line/Parts: | Process: | |

Observation Points:

Point

-free Engineering

-free

Big 3 Problem

Irrationality

Inconsistency

Waste

Use the Big 3 Memo to find observation points.

Present Condition

Date:

Observation:

After Improvements:

After Improvement

Date:

Improvement Points

Results

Cost Savings/Gain:

Suggestion No.

Grade:

5 minutes of careful observation . . .

BIG 3 MEMO

Write a memo whenever you see a problem

File No.

| Name: | Section: | Worksite: | Group: |

| Machine Type: | Line/Parts: | Process: |

Observation
Points:

Point

-free Engineering

-free

Big 3 Problem

Irrationality

Inconsistency

Waste

**Use the Big 3 Memo
to find observation
points.**

Present Condition

Date:

Observation:

After Improvements:

After Improvement

Date:

Improvement Points

Results

Suggestion No.

Cost Savings/Gain:

Grade:

5 minutes of careful observation . . .

BIG 3 MEMO

File No.

Write a memo whenever you see a problem

| Name: | Section: | Worksite: | Group: |

| Machine Type: | Line/Parts: | Process: |

Observation Points:

Point

-free Engineering

-free

Big 3 Problem

Irrationality

Inconsistency

Waste

Use the Big 3 Memo to find observation points.

Present Condition

Date:

Observation:

After Improvements:

After Improvement

Date:

Improvement Points

Results

Cost Savings/Gain:

Suggestion No.

Grade:

5 minutes of careful observation . . .

BIG 3 MEMO

File No.

Write a memo whenever you see a problem

Name:	Section:	Worksite:	Group:

Machine Type:	Line/Parts:	Process:

Observation
Points:

Point

-free Engineering

-free

Big 3 Problem

Irrationality

Inconsistency

Waste

Use the Big 3 Memo to find observation points.

Present Condition

Date:

Observation: _____

After Improvements: _____

After Improvement

Date:

Improvement Points

Results

Cost Savings/Gain:

Suggestion No.

Grade:

5 minutes of careful observation . . .

BIG 3 MEMO

Write a memo whenever you see a problem

File No.

Name:	Section:	Worksite:	Group:

Machine Type:	Line/Parts:	Process:

Observation Points:

Point

-free Engineering

-free

Big 3 Problem

Irrationality

Inconsistency

Waste

Use the Big 3 Memo to find observation points.

Present Condition

Date:

Observation:

After Improvements:

After Improvement

Date:

Improvement Points	**Results**	**Suggestion No.**
	Cost Savings/Gain:	Grade:

30

5 minutes of careful observation . . .

BIG 3 MEMO

File No.

Write a memo whenever you see a problem

| Name: | Section: | Worksite: | Group: |

| Machine Type: | Line/Parts: | Process: |

Observation Points:

Point

-free Engineering

-free

Big 3 Problem

Irrationality

Inconsistency

Waste

Use the Big 3 Memo to find observation points.

Present Condition

Date:

Observation:

After Improvements:

After Improvement

Date:

Improvement Points

Results

Cost Savings/Gain:

Suggestion No.

Grade:

5 minutes of careful observation . . .

BIG 3 MEMO

File No.

Write a memo whenever you see a problem

Name:	Section:	Worksite:	Group:

Machine Type:	Line/Parts:	Process:

Observation Points:

Point

-free Engineering

-free

Big 3 Problem

Irrationality

Inconsistency

Waste

Use the Big 3 Memo to find observation points.

Present Condition

Date:

Observation: _____

After Improvements: _____

After Improvement

Date:

Improvement Points

Results

Cost Savings/Gain:

Suggestion No.

Grade: